AFRICA QUEST SALT OF THE EARTH

YOHANNES TASSEW

DEDICATION

Africans who live and die for Africans!

PREFACE

CONTINENTAL CALL

Job title   -   Salt of the Earth

Department   -   As Per Your call of Soul

Location   -   Entire Africa

Sex   -   Male Salt of the Earth

                  -       Female Salt of the Earth

Salary   -   As per the Current Price of
                              Salt of the Earth

Qualification   - Unconditional Love and Holy Anger

Dear sons and daughters of Africa, from the day I post this vacancy till the end of the day in which the quest of Salt of the Earth comes to an end, I would like to let you know that You are mostly welcome to apply and I kindly request you to send me an envelope attached to pure love of motherland on it to the location mentioned above.

Sincerely Yours

Mama Africa

PROLOGUE

You are the salt of the earth .But if the salt loses its saltiness, how can it be made salty again? It is no longer good for anything, except to be thrown out and trampled underfoot.

You are the light of the world. A town built on a hill cannot be hidden. Neither do people light a lamp and put it under a bowl. Instead they put it on its stand, and it gives light to everyone in the house.

Matthew 5,-13-15

According to the vacancy released on various Media all over Africa by mama Africa, for her children at large. I have had an imaginary exclusive interview with her .And it's my pleasure to present you my stay in the following five chapters.

Pleasant reading…

Yohannes Tassew

CONTENTS

ACKNOWLEDGMENTS

For those who believe in me!

Make sure before you go through…

CHAPTER ONE

I feel honored for such a life time opportunity ever to meet you today Mama Africa and great pleasure for letting me have an exclusive interview and I thank you for your good will.

Am glad to meet you too, and be informed son, pleasure is all mine.

Wow! Just to get start with how old are you dear?

Oh! (Gorgeous smile) am getting old and older and am almost old as old as the earth itself.

Great Mama, let me directly proceed to the issue I get myself here today, it is public knowledge that you released such a unique continental call these days for your children. What makes you to do so?

Actually the root cause that drives me to do so has its grounds. It is not as such a specific reason, rather a very deep rooted cause in my entire life. Nevertheless, let me clarify you only the basic factors. One is deep-rooted and the other immediate one. You see am supposed to be big as big as my land square. But I found myself in very trilling situations, which made me very vexed and bothered about my destiny.

Leave alone my future but also my daily life became as dark as a midnight .Due to lack of children that could weep my tears and rely on as I am getting older and older. The people of the world pointed their fingers, how unfortunate I am, And consider me the continent that sleep billions of years in the bed of untapped, huge, natural and human resource. As an African mother, am nervous about my children.

One quest to save me and ones idea is making me fall. While one turns my Africanized civilization on, the other turns it off. Some weld power or use violence to make others obey and forced my land to experience miserable tragedies which leads to blood bath, Look at me, am not very well look after, am weak muscled, short sighted, contaminated, and abused fooled, enslaved.

They exploited me and my lands are eroded, degraded, polluted and generations are misdirected by my own children and other colonialists from Europe who came across far, far away. They say they came to me because of civilizing me but Commercial greed, territorial ambition, and political rivalry, all fuelled the European race to take over me.

Whatever they say why they came, as I was a magnificent and healthy land of unspeakable richness, I was sliced up like a cake. They scrambled me.

The scramble for Africa left me no alternative but remains me underdeveloped, misdirected and put me in the middle of nowhere.

Mama, I am afraid you are blaming them all for your failures? Don't you blame yourself? It seems a blame game?

I am not diverting the issue toward an external enemy. And am not seeking escape goats to blame my failing on. Am trying to show you how the external and internal enemies played me? It is not a blame game. But it is to trigger my children to rise again. It is not excuse for my fall. I know am not saying there is a curse on black people and curse on African continent.

As others say, lack of democracy for all the things has happened to me. It does not come out of the blue. There has to be some causes.

It is undeniable that there has been poor governance, corruption and mismanagement in my land. My failures are the result of my own children thoughts and actions. yet the legacy of colonialism, the support of the developed nations for repressive regimes in the Cold War, the creation of the debt trap, the massive failure of Structural Adjustment Program imposed by the IMF and World Bank and the deeply unfair rules on international trade played me most.

The role of the developed nations in creating the conditions for Africa's crisis cannot be denied. Its overriding responsibility must be to put its own house in order, and to end the unjust policies that are inhibiting my development. Not blaming them blindly on my failures. In fact, there influence crippled me.

If I could be conscious and able to lock my door before, they couldn't come in through. My incapability to protect and defense their thoughts and actions were fragile and weak. It's undeniable. But remember they are uninvited guests to my land. Gate crashers!! Who rip and rape me? Both my children and outsider shred and slit me.

I think scramble for Africa has left quite a lot, Like that of education, health care and development? Don't you think?

The scramble left me education for underdevelopment. They used education as one institution in forming slaves. They used my children to shoulder white man's burden of civilizing. Even the little infrastructures they created were for their own advantages. It was for their luxuries in my land. They compensated their poor life back there home. They make me a mother, which came last in my own home after them. Maternity and sanitations services were geared towards the well being of the white settler's. They exploit my minerals irresponsibly. They made huge profit and received great, social service, under colonialism. They left me uneducated.

My previous development was blunted, halted and turned back. As a mother, I had a power over my children and home land but I lost my power. I was forced .I found myself forced, in a situation to relinquish my power to them. That in itself is a form of underdevelopment. I was supposed to have my own Africanized form of development. I couldn't train or educate my children in my own interest. Rather ceased to set indigenous cultural goals and standards.

The invention of tradition undertaking in my land finally resulted the thrown of many societies of mine in to disarray of a new order.

Put aside my custom, culture, tradition and norms and follow their new road. My cultures were almost erased. Their education and civilizing programs gave me only a minority skill and set that served their interest. Skills to produce sugar cane not help me to produce sugar out of it. You know the power to act independently is guarantee to participate actively and consciously in history, but I was removed from it (history). I couldn't make history. They put me in no more maker of history. We were beetle objects to be looked at under a microscope and examined for unusual features. I was forced to use my brain, thinks as their wish; my mouse speaks on behalf of them and my hands works for their greedy interest. How can I be a stranger to my own land? Rather made me feel and act as a second citizen, who has no any right to do things in an African manner and advanced Africanized form of civilization.

I could not have a single state flourish. Almost all my states and kingdoms were removed altogether. Even those that appeared to survive were nothing but puppet creations. Though, they were hated and despised such colonial stooges in my face, they bitter my land serving against me and for colonials. In most of my land, most colonial administrators did not have the manpower or resources to fully administer my land and had to rely on my local power structure, to help them, not to help me. Various functions and groups within my societies exploited these European requirements for their own purposes. My children attempted to gain position of power, within communities, by cooperating with Europeans. It is heartbreaking. You know it's better to be stubbed by your enemies than your own children. Women were treated like beasts of burden. Colonialism blocked the further evolution of national solidarity. I was strained to rep divide and rule, tribal conflict and border conflict. Because of, they plough and saw the value of stimulating the internal tribal jealousies. Put me lost class solidarity.

 My land has become an attractive and profitable dumping ground for nations and arm manufacturers, eager to get rid of weapon stocks made superfluous by the end of the Cold war. By technological developments Throughout the Cold War, major powers such as the U.S.A, the Soviet Union and others supported various African regimes and dictatorships. Their extended hand some possibly promising leaders in the early days of the independence movements throughout the Third World were overthrown. There was disregard from the major powers as to how this would affect my land and the people, over a billion worth of weapons to my land has come from the U.S alone, according to a report from the World Policy Institute, despite the fact that, Europe for example, was able to " exploit my resources" to help rebuild after World War II. The proliferation of small arms in the region, when the Cold War ended has helped fuel many conflicts. My profit was that of, wars, religious contentions, clashes of political expansion, tribalism.

To counter this tribalism some of my African leaders proclaimed the single party state to be the only means to control the excessive, ethnically based competition for the global goods of modernity — education, health, and the eradication of poverty. Competitive democracy they said would only lead to poverty. Yet one-party rule unrestrained by the moral check of shared community had the same result. It proved to be a mask for oppression, ethnocracy and kleptocracy. Tribalism entrenches regional separation. I was partitioned in to racial blocks. Its effect on bringing together many different ethnic people within a nation that did not reflect not have (in such a short period of time) the ability to accommodate or provide for, the cultural and ethnic diversity. More over its artificial boundaries created in my land has devastating impact. Its impact still bothers me like a time bomb; Becomes means to continual conflict within. Even if you see recently what the world, my children and others get me more of my time. Wars without the involvement of the Western nations do not seem newsworthy enough to appear on international media news agendas, and the little coverage given only focuses on the brutality of the conflict and not on possible solutions.

Son should I cross my arm and wait till international media give me huge coverage and solutions to my problems?

NO, I SHALL BE VOICE LOUD AND CALL MY OWN CHILDREN to give me for an African problem an African solution. The magnitude of my problem requires an urgent and timely solution. And I believe I have the right to be heard. Nature gave me all sort of situation to contain with. I have always two path ways,

TO DO or NOT TO DO

I run away as well face the situations all the time. I could come through the easy and hard route in front of me. I have a misery of hardships as well you know, EVERY SITUATION TESTED ME!!

Its public knowledge many situations have tested you. Today I will let you be specific about it, at least the irritating or frustrating ones? Please take your time.

Beside the devastating natural difficulties like those of - volcanic eruptions, weather events ,hurricanes, cyclones, earthquakes, floods and flash floods, and locust infestation. Moreover famines, droughts (Sahel drought) and flood crisis. Every year a variety of disasters occurred and these are becoming more prevalent. Disaster frequency is increasing. My land is under the greatest threat from natural disasters. Disasters, notably droughts, claimed many victims.

Though I have the potential to feed the world as a whole, I have experienced the highest recorded number of disaster events for the past years. Recovery from economic loss could not be recouped because of stunted growth and other internal problems in me. I expect more hardship await me ahead as well, unless I got to do something serious about it. I mean some strategies to mitigate the problem of natural hazards.

Every situation tested me. Leave alone the natural disasters occurred in my entire life, from the time of my childhood, I have submit myself to myriad wars, civil wars, colonial war, war of independence, separatist conflict, riots, massacres. All these and others tested me, Oh dear Son; I came all the way through... Cemetery, Hykoss, Bitterlakes, Esarhaddon, Pelusium, Caesar, Great Abbasid, Mahdist, Suez, Attrition, Yom Kippur, Berber, Ifri, Rif, Zaian, Gao, Timbuktu, Taghaza, Melila, Almoravid-Almohad, Almohad-Marinid, Darfur, Punic, Jugurthine, Vandals, Guntharic, Maghreb, Operation Dignity, Carthage, vandals, Vandalic, Mourish, Bizerte, Fall of Tlemcen, Pacification, Setifand Guelma, Sand, Westernsahara, Kush, Punt, Adal, al-Shabaab, Ifat's, Adal , Shimbrakyah, Shart, Bacente, Jarte, Wofla, Wayna Daga, Adwa, Amba Alagi , Coalit, Anjovan, Grand Port, Interahamwe(Rwandian genocide) , Burundi Genocide, Titanic express, Itaba, Gatumba, Operation Entebbe, Mau Mau , Shifa, Garissa, Wagalla , Turbi village, Abomey(Dahomey) , Oyo-Dahomey, Ashanti-Akim, Yourba-Ashanti ,Dahomey, Holy Spirit Movement, Agacher strip, Fulani,Fula Jihads, Mandingo, Anglo-Ashanti, Golden Stool, Accra riots, Guinea-Bissau, Liberian, Sandaki Usurpation, Mossiraid, Tuareg, Maptj jihad, Agacher strip, Agawad , Songhai , Kaocen, Azawad,

Fulani, Fula Jihads, Rafin Jaki Jihad, Boko Haram, Batepa, Action ,Ndogboyosoi, Ifni, Bush, Brazzavile, lord's Resistance Army, Simba, Shaba, Ituri, Kivu, ADF, Robih, Napaleonic, Nawandwe-Zulu, Great Trek, Weenen, Anglo-Zulu, Xhosa, Maritz, Sharpeville, Soweto, Matabele, Chimurenga/Rhodesion Bush , Boer , Gun , Mozambican , Angolan , Caprivi , Herero , Trans Sahara, Mount Elgan. I can't count each and every trouble I had encountered and undertaking whilst talking to you right now, numerous situations have tested me. Wuhu …

"GOOD GOD ABOVE!"

"OH MY GOD", I can't believe you came up through these entire?

Oh son, I can't judge the rest of the world whatever they say about me. It is anticipated since it is my real story. You know what they call me?

The theater of war!!
Rebuilding from the theater of war has been tough and unfinished struggle for me.

Oh mama don't be nervous about what tested you all along .At least you should be happy being free of

colonialism. You have earned freedom from imperial powers. Was not it enough to make you happy?

Oh son yes indeed, I am happy about it thanks   for my children of Pan Africans. I am independent physically now. But you see, even as colonial administrators parted, they left behind supportive elites, in effect, continued the shop honing of my wealth, am suffering the impacts and the juice of its legacy at a time. The freedom from imperial powers was, and is still, not a smooth transition. I always thought my feeling about it. Yes am happy, colonialism in the traditional sense may have ended, but the end result are much the same. For instance, let me show you how it is difficult for me. It put me in unequal international trade and comparative disadvantage.

International trade and economic arrangements have done little to benefit my people and me .it has further exacerbated my problem.Thus, the continuing colonial arrangement made me not walk long in the long walk to economic freedom. Structural adjustments have aggressively opened up my land with devastating effect, including the requirement to cut back on health, education and public service and so on. If you see the AID and DEBT I receive from them, made me crippled.

The immense burden of debt has further crippled my ability to develop. Even the aid I receive has a precondition. Why not I feel nervous and unhappy? They made me one who go out for shopping and has no penny in pocket. They already took it. Even the left wealth I have still is going directly and indirectly. I am the image of poverty. My leaders and their fellows send billions of dollars to foreign banks selfishly. They collect from the mass and other means in the mask of benefiting the mass but use it personal comfort.

At the mask of the mass creating mess becomes normal to my messed up leaders. Greed and unconsciousness drives them to steel and rob from their own pocket. Leadership is working to comfort others not oneself.

I can't make my own history in my land by my own children shoulders. There shall not be shortcut to happiness. Even my children try to fool me, pretend as loyal servant, as nationalists, liberators, Freedom fighter. At the same time forget all about me. What my children do on behalf of me is embracing and shameful act to me.

How shameful you feel, am trying to get more of it, would you clarify me a bit more?

The scare all over my body reminds me to continue the pathways that do not agreed with my hearts compass. I got myself pity. Had not I been pioneer mother to ancient civilization of the world? They call me a mother of 3rd world. I have had enough of this miserable life. I can't count how many times I heard why they mock at me and say: - TIA!! (This is Africa.)I can't count how many times I feel ashamed of my dependency on the rest of the world. Especially, the haves .Cannot count on how many times I feel ashamed of how I am hammered and stoned by my own children and others.

How many days and nights I wept of not self sufficiency. And wonder how frequently listen my children told themselves, how stupid and cursed they are and felt ashamed and despair because am their mother and because they are Africans. Sometimes I think and wonder why it took me dozen of years to accomplish peace, development and an African mood of civilization, like that of civilization I had before contacting Europe.

Out of the limitations that the negative attitude has imposed me in the past, the one which pains me is not having able to secure my children self food sufficiency and identity crisis. Another of my frustration has had to abandon my own mood of civilization and more recently forced, tapped, baptized by the waste of western civilization, which imposed huge identity crisis over. You know ,my children pits me being recipient of only the waste of western civilization not even try to catch the fruits of it, the good side of western civilization.

I was the land and homes of both Islam and Christianity almost from their very inception, but nowadays they crashed one another due to an extremism point of view of oneself. My feminine honor has been demoralized being robbed and had group rape. But now I say NO MORE PAIN! I had enough.

I no more hear cry of starving children scream of woman, misery of humanity and sorrows of civil war. Don't want to be a theatre of war no more. I need to be different, am supposed to be unique and disserve transformation, breakthrough, paradigm shift and change. Do put all my challenges behind me, no more going to carry the spit of curse. No more to wear a towel of disaster made of misery and customized with negativity.

Due to my famine and drought that made me well known by the entire world. I Am nervous felt grievance and remain grounded. But now am no more supposed to count when my children ashamed of being an AFRICAN! So I came out to communicate them as a parent about their thoughts and actions. Want to be parent who uses its heart as mirrors for my children to see themselves and augment their development, lift everyone's spirits. So long as am rich enough of children over approximately to relay on my children.

No matter how bad Europeans scrambled me ,no matter

how I was side steeping life challenges, I always remember myself one day I will have my own African children who can make my heart shine. And will choose and agree to follow my hearts compass. Therefore, this is the time to transform and lean on my own children.

Nature treats all my children fairly, bestowing a role and mission to be fulfilled in the specific period to each of my children. So, am being sick and tired of being an ashtray of poor leadership. Because as a mother, I will not advance rather perish, if I don't have salt of the earth among my children, who generate opportunity for all of them to achieve life calling; and that is why am badly in search of the one.

The one who dwell not in negativity and darkness, thanks much on good things and righteous. Am loud enough to call and have someone who can be salt of my earth. I feel uneasy so I opt for silence no more.

No more public execution to my servant leaders in every square. I know I have a stroke of luck and encountered with the evil actions of my children over one another. They were vanished by all the lies invented to discredit them. I didn't benefit from industrial revolution for I was subjugated at the time was reduced to slaves and indentured servants. Was robed, my identity, dignity, self worth and self respect.

My people are products of oppression. And have had instilled in them or us a sense of timidity, and spirit of dependency. But I shall accent no more. And I am eager and committed to quest Salt of the Earth.

CHAPTER TWO

May I see the big picture of what you are Questing as Salt of the Earth? What do you mean by that?

I failed in many cases to realize the capacity of the leadership potential within us or me. I had illusions that the road to dignity for my people would be extremely long. Along with, I am tired to be led by the relentless policy pursued by outsiders. I have accepted all the outsiders told me to do and found my problem getting worse, never my wound nor my pain healed, rather their prescription results overdose on me and my children. The outsiders" TO DO LIST never seem to end. It's endless.

Now days I cannot resist the temptation of shameful feeling I am having, receiving of economic aid. Though it gives me temporary solutions for my deep rooted problem, never is permanent solution to me. Somewhat felt crippled and parasite. I kept myself busy of leading my life at the direction of the donors or advanced people. I am unable to lead my life as my heart desire. I felt disability. However, I am convinced that disability is not inability. Yes it is undeniable am in need of help but whilst I try to stand firm by myself, feel incompetent and lacks faith in me, plus all these dependency lead me to unwanted psychological trauma. I wonder about myself, How came Mama Africa with unspeakable richness can't solve her own problem? Especially at time of receiving aids with many fold preconditions from the donor to satisfy their request and solve my complicated problem temporarily, I fail in to vacillating mood, and found myself in the middle of nowhere. fearful of rejecting those hands which were there for me at time of my need, and refusing not to accept their policy offers results uneasy consequences but for how long I kept my self silent and remain recipient of outsiders relentless offers?

The clock is ticking. The world is moving forward and I remain tail of the world. Time pass and life goes on, by then, I came up with a decision to face the consequence than staring forever my eyes and stretching my empty hands to the develop world. Subsequently, I found myself in need of someone, among my children who have no chimera and determined to make the road of African dignity very short.

Prescription formed within for my problem, address it accordingly is my dream.   I call for Someone who understand what is happening on the ground and why. Prescribe the right solution within, no matter what its consequences are.   Because only the wearer know where the shoe pinches.

Now a day's am voracious to have someone that can make my life his life and my death as its own. I badly need the very courageous leader that would make my land prosperous and bless my people lives. I am questing leaders among my children who are servant leaders, in which their unselfish service bless all the mountains, lands, lakes, rivers, all living and non living things in my land. Make me favorite place for investment and change the existing image of Africa as investment risk and dumping grounds for cheap industrial products.

The people who live from north to south and from east to west up to central shall be transformed to prosperity. To make all these happen requires remarkable leader. the one who wear very balanced eye glass, that contains positive African attitude; to see all my children who have been robbed of the opportunity and right to discover their true potential due to oppressive and incapacitating ideologies' and systems. Those children of mine who have been impacted the physical and mental damage inflated on their self concept, self worth and self-esteem. I mean it. I need someone among my children to became salt of the earth and let my people to freely speak ,argue ,discuss to share their experience, aspirations , destinies and hopes in the interest of Mother Africa.

I call for my children who can iodize my land and keen on to have a very gifted person who can be enormous ingredients of life for the people at hand. Need African leader that can sustain my own unique features of cultures. These cultures of mine have value. My Children must understand this value and never surrender again to the invention of traditions, because   features of my cultures cannot be eclipsed by other cultures, are not really comparable phenomena. Then I will be glad to have one within who can lay the foundation of renaissances for the future generation. As a mother, I long for to be seen well dressed, and well fed, well protected at the land of prosperity which I can imagine myself enjoy the yoke of life together with my grandchildren.

Questing for the light of my land, which brighten me and look for the missing ingredient? Salt of the Earth protect my infant economy, from the chill winds of the financial gales. Had I had salt of the earth that is courageous to protect me, as they protect their own and prevent mine? I quest my own children to untie me from the economic system which I am not in control of.

I would have been able to be competitive, in international trade and benefit equally. Salt of the earth is someone who can give my children an idea about product and productivity, show them to transform from Backwardness to Modernization and how to produce from the raw material at hand. Some assumed me a complete savage and incapable of developing my resources myself .and present me policy of not my heart desire to exploit me again. But I know I can, have faith in my children, feel it is the time to start, and became self sufficient, through the leadership of African salt of the earth. Great leadership knows where and how to seize opportunities.

The great leadership of salt of the earth that I quest includes the capacity to influence, inspire rally, direct, encourage, motivate, induce, move, mobilize and activate my children and others to pursue my heart desire to be well civilized and prospered continent.

Salt of the earth's leadership pilot its service with commitment, momentum, confidence and courage. Salt of the earth systematize all the resources available, be it human power or natural resources' and coordinate in a very smart way to meet my wish and need, Never close their eyes, to bring all my dreams come true. I want to enjoy my sovereign existence and necessitate my children to fully control our own African affairs and destinies.

The very single step walks of salt of the earth accompanied, great responsibility and accountability. So my children shall be responsible and accountable of their service, if wished to be light of my land.

Simply put, I quest my children to be the light of the world. Here let me remember you what the holy bible says: "You are the light of the world. A town built on a hill cannot be hidden. Neither do people light a lamp and put it under a bowel. Instead they put it on its stand, and it gives light to everyone in the house." My quest is to contain children who can be selfless servant to my people. Salt of the Earth means servant of the people. My leaders should understand and internalize leadership, as selfless service to the people. Mobilize my people and rally around to change my weakness in to strength. Let me tell you, saying of Prophet Muhammad (bpuh): - "the leader of people is their servant".

Although leadership is the ability to obtain followers, the service of Salt of the Earth goes beyond obtaining followers. Salt of the Earth do not go after a position, rank or title or status. It is being the person others will gladly and confidently follow. It is being highly influential person to bless. It would be great to remind you what the most influential leader of all the time responded, when asked how to become a great leader: - Who is that and what he responded mama?

He is the young master teacher Jesus Christ and responded;-

"Whoever, wants to become great among you must be your servant,... just as the Son of Man did not come to be served, but to serve, and to give his life as a ransom for many."

So does mama Africa quest great leader. True leaders to serve my people and not to be served, I am tired of African leaders, who are obsessed with ethnocracy and kleptocracy. No matter how big or small the social status they have. Whatever their language and color is, whatever their tribe and race they belong or have originated. Salt of the Earth are happy to help people to grow personally. To speak their minds openly based on their own free will.

Think all Africans as one.

Even though every single individual has its own belief, tradition, races, where one origins and tribe that belongs, but all are human beings created at the image and likeliness of God at the land of Africa. It is necessary to understand the true value of a single individual in true leadership, and knows individuals who are personally grown can make a difference, individually and collectively as two hands makes a light work. Through selfless service touches people's heart. Because the real address of a true leader is people's heart.

Salt of the Earth produce much followers as well leaders'. For the most part, produce leaders.

My leadership vacuum seems not easily or quickly be filled. Whereas, salt of the earth take the initiative to fill the leadership vacuum that, Mama Africa faced for long. Exerts high influence and takes other influencers among the people to the higher levels. Salt of the Earth lead others to be salt of the earth. To leads people, true leader love and care before, never try to lead people without loving them. Motivate people to try to win life.

Relatively speaking, my people work hard but are not productive as needed. Thus, I quest leader who teaches and direct them the wisdom of working hard and also how smart they work to achieve African unity based on economic integration. And propound to start and support all the necessary efforts directed towards the eradication of poverty. Therefore, I quest for salt of the earth to relief and cure my nonstop pain and heal my growing wound. I believe, almost every soul of Africa is brutally disturbed by the unlimited conflict or civil war.

Salt of the earth will, instill my people the passion and wisdom to know and cultivate certain valuable attitude about everything. They will offer us the mind set as I quest, develop my African leadership potential to the fullest and fulfill what my people were born to be.

Salt of the earth will adjust my people's ways of thinking. My African people are derived to live by others philosophies not African philosophy. Forced to live others thought and convictions. Our philosophies determine the way we think. In fact we live our thoughts and manifest them in our attitudes towards ourselves and others. We cannot live beyond our thoughts and convictions. But my people are conditioned in dependency. Receptive of others thought philosophy, idea cultures, traditions and ways of living. Due to this and other factors, my people are manifesting not the original African form of civilization rather others. And its effects are getting worse.

We must be responsible to our attitude. Taking in to consideration this fact, salt of the earth exerts its influence power to make my leaders at every level more accountable to their own people than the outside world. This is because my renaissance can only came from within me and it must be spearheading by Africans at every level.

Our attitude needs to be reentered and renewed as my heart desire. And it shall come true by the great selfless service of great son of Africa. That is Africa Salt of the Earth, a highly influential and beloved leader. Because, Leadership equals to influence and influence is the essence of leadership.

Salt of the earth of my heart desire influence my people how to do things within. Leaders of my heart desire can build my people follow or go willingly beyond their stated authority. They own the ability to make people to work for them, towards a common goal, once they are not obligated. Salt of the earth care for people, love people develop people. Believe in people development. Not only this, they coach and inspire the people, Develop my children to do the work which I dream to achieve. Induce the spirit of change among my people. Be it qualified, unqualified, be it literate or illiterate.

Develop my people to achieve African unity based on economic integration and political unification. Salt of the Earth think for the people, Love and work for them. They live within them. Invest time with. Have integrity, courage and nothing to fear. Never hesitate to face the different political forms which were not my heart desire nevertheless I have experimented and resulted in conflict and continuous violence among my children. Salt of the earth never fear to emancipate my children from populist dictatorship and tribalism and unfair wealth distribution.

It is public knowledge that my children looted my wealth and kept me impoverished. However it is up to salt of the earth and my people to maintain the economic injustice and pressure the separation of power and maintain democratic limitations of the exercise of governmental power.

Exerts unconditional love among them and stop the manipulation of the poor by the rich. Convince and act my rich children to equip my poor children to rival. Bridge the entire gaps that exist. This is because economic development is necessary for political instability. It is time for Africans to dry the sources of military force against unarmed people by African leaders. I quest my children to root out corruption and miss management.

Every step of salt of the earth accompanies compassion with good will. They are enthusiastic, not self centered. They live and die for the vision they see for Mama Africa. No matter how hard the leadership process might be to civilize, develop and light my life, constantly strives to keep my people integrity intact. It pits me almost all of my children came to power to serve me with compassion and ended up by becoming corrupt. Even those of my leaders who came to power by overthrowing which they believe corrupt and undemocratic, ended up sucking blood and manipulative than they had replaced. Servant leaders create positive change. Understands the negativity in my land and changes in to positivity.

They are positive minded and has good understanding of people. Never pretend, are man of their word, their yes is yes and their no is no. have strong and firm stand to Africans prosperity, Stay exemplary of all times.

Remain pioneer in positive thoughts and actions for me. They make personal changes before asking my people to change. They give what they have. You know we cannot give what we don't have, Understands my history well enough. They are acquainted with how to offer ownership of change to others. They Propound and flourish the spirit of Africa. Expose my children and leaders at any level to common problems and shape their attitudes collectively to seek solutions to the existing problems within.

They propound the idea of or the true essence of African Salt of the Earth is to speak aloud, speak for oneself and to decide our own destiny and master our own fate. Craft the road map to be strong and to speak in unity within and in world affairs. Salt of the Earth recognize first my people need to change their perspectives not there problems. Salt of the earth main job is to change my people's thoughts and behaviors. Our attitude is our attitude. True leaders know a problem is something one can do something about. Salt of the earth have the right attitude, the original African attitude, which is uncontaminated African ways of thinking. Mentor my peoples to be responsible to their attitudes.

Attitudes are the most important assets. There is nothing as powerful as attitude. My people past life and decision have formed their present attitude. My children are strained not to live like the present need of Africans attitude. Bear in mind this; salt of the earth strive to adjust my people mind set based on African philosophy.

Its leadership must condition my people mental to function in form of true African identity to determine their interpretations of and response to their environments. Attitude creates your world and designs your destiny. I was required to have an attitude of slavery thinks as slaves not as humans.

I was like guest in my own homeland. Felt bound and restricted. I was not in charge of my life. My history witnessed I was dominated. Circumstances dominated me for long. Be it physical, spiritual or psychological.

We were forced to live under conditions. Though I am human being with different colors, am ignored as I am not cradle of human being. I was not designed to live under these conditions. I was forced to be gust in my own land. I was designed to be able to manage my environment, but I couldn't make it.

I expect Africans Salt of the Earth will have some unique attitude to manage my environment. So, my leaders need to be one step ahead of the people that distinguish from them. Attitude of a salt of the earth produce certain behaviors that stretch African leadership beyond the limitation of the norm. Salt of the earth fight the emancipation from negative and contaminated attitudes domination of my people, Find ways and menses of ameliorating the dilemma of Africans under African domination and racial discrimination within us. I quest for African salt of the earth to liberate me from single tribe domination.

Selfless service is a source of inspiration to African emancipation. You need to contain vast opportunity to my people to express, their economic, political and social aspirations. Africans leaders should Originate, recognize then implements primary African principles that African should developed for Africans. I quest need my children redeem me from the scourge of tribalism.

I quest for salt of the earth because I am tired of corrupt political system and government. Ethnocracy or Kleptocracy is giving me savior headache. I am feeling hysterically pain.

Leadership equals to influence and influence is the essence of leadership.

Mama, don't consider me, pointing my fingers as they did to you, how come you can't have it. Out of approximately over one billion children of you, if it means such a servant leader? Hadn't you such a leader at all?

Oh you know what the thing is very strange. Of course, I had few of them, but my people said to them you are no more good for nothing and thrown out and trampled under their foot. Mocked at them Ridiculed and Humiliated in public, were given bullet to their head and rope to their neck. Some of them has lost there foot print, no idea where they were taken. Though they took them alive, even there course never came back. Half of them migrated, flew away my land, thereby saving their skin. The eagle of death grabbed few others OF MY SALT OF THE EARTH. Nature has its way.

What could I do? Has found dead in office and faced unnatural death, some were forced to melt down their courage. Imprisonment darken there heart. Due to lack of persistence and endurance on seasonal storm on the ship of servant leadership, some of my Salt of the Earth had pulled over themselves, from the ship of servant leadership voluntarily.

The rest were fragile and their leadership was much distorted. They were corrupted; they abuse and misuse their power. And my children became dictators and hypocrites. They sack my children's blood and roost their skins. Others were ignorant and had hidden agendas behind their leadership. There hidden inconsistencies were exposed. Their attitudes are very negative and narrow minded by will. As well as, are disrespectful of my people and voracious to enjoy the prize of leadership and refrain from paying its price. They had been intolerant of differences and unable to see out of the box. Only fraud, intimidation, pressure and coercive power was there methods to do whatever they want to do in my land. Not having a clear and understandable and locally or adapted ideologies. Rather they brought ideologies, from the rest of the world and take it for granted and applied it as is. They were not independent thinkers. And I can say they followed worn -out principles. Still I don't have a heart to say I had leaders as of my heart desire.

Love of power and money made others to intoxicate and stabbed them. Enormous self service hanged them in fact; they were supposed to be selfless servants for my children to bless my land, but they couldn't make it. Where the hell should I go witnessing this in my bare eye at my land?

Moreover, this for how long I get beaten my breast by my own children who fed it , for how long I kept quite while my children who I fed my breast stubbed my side, it breaks my heart. It's better to be stubbed by enemy than your child. It pits me for long. My shoulder is no stronger enough neither to smell their negativity nor carry their spit of curse. Of course, still I have few of them who attempt to do their best and crawl to stand upright on the road of new era.

Never then, you can neither clap by a single hand nor plough a land by a fox. Rather Salt of the Earth obliges the art of winning peoples heart. Enlarge its wisdom to influence others and make, the rest to follow your path in order to saltine my life and iodize my body and bless my soul. Therefore, missing many of my ingredients of life, I won't sit and cross my arm waiting to see them drop from a tree of mango as ripe mango and remain silent till my day come, I know nothing is free ,I cannot get something for nothing. I immediately and wisely exert my effort to be able to have adequate Salt of the Earth among my children, shall not be destined to remain loyal to poverty. Rather it's time for me to call my children within and outside .Questing... I am left with a reeking trail of their blood.

My eyes have seen the decapitated heads of my leaders in different level. Their arms and legs were cut off by the order Of the dictators and their bodies and cars had been riddled with bullets, and had been tortured and killed.

Ok, mama, I can say those of your leaders had been strived their best to serve you, they strived as much as they can. And no matter what happened on many of them, were forced to stop there service and others served you in different direction of your heart desire. I can understand that, but what about other people of you? Why do you think they remain silent or avoid leadership responsibility? Why children of Africa don't dare to do so?

People think that they are not good enough to be leaders. Some of my people think they are not morally up to the standard of leadership. Others think that they have no leadership qualities. Others feel that they have too many personal problems to become leaders. They cannot imagine being saddled with other people's problems.

My children convince themselves, that they are not good enough to be leaders. Being a leader does not mean being perfect. You do not have to be perfect to become a leader. If that were the case, then there would be no leaders in the world at all.

This does not mean that there are no standards. GOD expects the highest standards of character and morality. And yet, he works with imperfect people. GOD looks at the heart. So does mama Africa. What you need is to make sure that your heart is right. We all are capable of leadership. But our leadership role differs as our life's call varies. My children need to understand, no one is perfect. Jesus works with imperfect disciples. They were neither self actualized nor righteous. Or uniquely blessed and chosen, due to their specialty.

They are summoned, and changed their mind, not to think and act as before. Accepted the call to be Salt of the Earth, start to think and act differently and made difference. Though they were not good enough to be leaders, didn't avoid the leadership responsibility. If there is a will, there is always a way. My children lack good will and avoid leadership responsibility thinking that they are not good enough to be leaders. Others of their avoidance are Many of my people do not know that they are leaders. They do not know because no one has told them so! They don't even know that they have the ability to lead. Some people think that only a few people are born to lead, the rest to follow.

As I told you my children are crawling in the swamp of identity crisis. They don't know why they are here on earth. I believe here we are on earth for something special mission. Here we are designed to rule over every living creature, rule over the fish of the sea and the birds of the air, over the livestock, over all the earth and over all the creatures that moves along the ground. To understand oneself, one must understand the principles established in these words. It deeply embedded in the nature of man. Still, my children may not know that they are leader. Few ask, most never.

 Remember you don't get if you don't ask!!And beside my children don't know that they are leaders because they are not told who truly they are, they are in identity crisis. They are misdirected. They are not well educated and well crafted.

The education of civilizing through colonization formatted my children's brain to think indifferent arena. Not their true identity, so that they remain dependent generations. My African children's think and act about their true identity differently, not even close to Africans way.

In addition, almost all of my children are not prepared to pay the price to become leaders. They did not want to be a leader in a certain ways. Are a quiet person and that enjoyed their privacy. Becoming a leader will cost you your valued life. They don't want to lose private life. They

Are busy as busy as a bee discussing about the fancy world, western entertainments, crazy about HOLLYWOOD and BOLYWOOD, not even close to AFRO WOOD! , discussed in people's homes and cars. Like all leaders, my children do not want to be praised by some and criticized by others. This is the lot of a leader. This is why some people turn away from leadership. True leadership involves sacrifice. People do not want to end up disgraced and hated as many African prominent leaders have been. As I told you earlier, there are many leaders who have ended up in disgrace after taking up the mantle of leadership. Others have experienced terrible hurts and had bitter experiences. Some have been crucified by the people they led. My children watched how leaders have been rewarded with evil after many years of service.

I Have seen several (and I mean almost all) governments throw out their leader after one has led them for many years. Have seen leaders ridiculed and humiliated by members they have ministered to, for years and at great expense in my land. I have seen several Heads of State came to unnatural deaths after ruling the nation for some years. We have seen leaders being murdered in cold blood after delivering judgments they thought were right. The fear of pains of being in leadership makes my children to refuse.

Who then would like to be a leader in such an environment?

Oh son am afraid you are misunderstood somewhat, environment is just everything that surrounds us, we as humans, as the precious hand work of god, we were suppose to control, rule over our environment ,but what is happening in my land is the opposite. Our environment controlling us, we shall never let our environment shape us. Rather we better rule over our environment. It is our responsibility to change such an environment. We all are responsible to do so. If we do so our greatness shall comes so. Please bear in mind that the price of African greatness is responsibility of my children. It is time to remember what Plato says: - "HE WHO REFUSES TO RULE IS LIABLE TO BE RULED BY ONE WHO IS WORSE THAN HIMSELF. "

When you study the fate of the leaders around, it is only natural that people shun leadership and choose a quiet life of peace and anonymity. I can understand why somebody would stay away from the entire world of lying politicians and corrupt leadership. But avoiding and refraining never be the right solution for mama Africa. Though avoiding responsibility is not the solution, people fear that they will be accused and hated. They do not want to end up disgraced and hated as many prominent leaders have been.

Leaders are often accused of being ambitious. They are often accused of having bad motives. I know some people accuse them of being in the leadership for money and personal prestige. And that's why they remain silent and avoid African leadership responsibility directly and indirectly.

The major reasons people avoid responsibility is that they think they'll look dumb or incompetent or that they'll be punished in some way. If our leadership culture and political culture is set up to hurt or shame people then, naturally avoid accepting responsibility for their actions.

On the other hand, the new generation shall promote an African philosophy where people are encouraged to learn from their mistakes, made them to be more open to evaluating and improving their behavior. At last but not the list, most people are too selfish to be leaders. Leadership is selfless service, not serving oneself. Most people are too selfish to be leaders. Such people care only about themselves. Yes we all love ourselves. We do well for self and care about us. That is natural. And that's true. But they don't desire to understand the essence of true life through serving others.

Life in serving others offers meaningful life and pleasure. They are happy to have self food efficiency and comfort. They are happy to have the peace and democracy. They are happy to have prosperity. But they couldn't care less about anybody else.

"Once I am okay," they think, "Everything is okay." That is a spirit of selfishness. This spirit challenges the spirit of African unity and harmony.

Our connectedness's, for a common cause are in danger. A selfish person cannot be bothered to go through any training or sacrifice to become a leader. He will not pay out any energy to help another soul.

Expending energy to help others soul inquires one to master oneself first. I know it's hard to master oneself but possible. Prophet Muhammad (pbuh) said:-the greatest war is not jihad, but the war with oneself. Not being too selfish requires war within. If you win over yourself first, then there it comes to be there for my people to win over their life. The discovery of self is the birth of leadership. Did my children win over themselves?

Some of us can not even get out of bed. Therefore, most of my people are too selfish to be leaders. My children shall rebuke that spirit of laziness and selfishness. Unless and otherwise, mama Africa remain ridiculed and laughed at.

Opt no silence, I feel agitated and uneasy. Whatever they say they avoid leadership responsibility, life is a choice we all make every day. Yet, I am influencing them highly to be influential children and became my Salt of the Earth. In view of the fact, that leadership is the exercise of influence for a common cause.

You said salt of the earth is all about influence, and is the essence of Leadership.
What is influence?

To be an effective leader, it is necessary to influence others, to support and implement decisions that the leader and group members perceive as necessary. Without influence, leadership does not occur. In other words, leadership is the act of influencing outcomes. The major role of a leader is to change people's thought attitude and behavior.

Life is influence.

Everything we do (and don't do) leaves an impression. The major role of a leader is to change people thought, attitude and behavior. I understand influence as the ability to persuade others (rather than force or coerce) to think and/or act in a certain way. Saying that influence is to effect someone else's or groups thoughts, feelings and behavior such that they conform to your end goal for better or worse. In addition to that, influence is anything that brings about a change in our actions or thoughts. Influence is the ability to cause desirable and measurable actions and outcomes. It is making people WANT to do what YOU want them to do.

 Opening my children's mind to different possibilities and expanding their potential. I could say influence is anything that brings about a change in our actions or thoughts. Influence is what drives one's senses to do what, otherwise may not be possible. As you can see my people are tattooed their mind in "impossible attitude" and live like unproductive and irresponsible manner to their own and their continent prosperity. Prefers to migrate or fly away to the land of opportunity. "THIREATTITUDE", influence is the ability to put a complex concept into simple words. This in turn, makes it easy for the mass to understand.

Influence is the ability of a person to indirectly help or cause another person to make a decision or take an action. Influence involves the subtle persuasion of others to, do, act or say, what another wants them to do with no coercion.

The ability to motivate others to do as you would base on their trust and belief in you. My point of view of influence is anything that has the power to change the course of direction in any area of thought. Influence is the ability to empower and initiate change.

We all have our circle of influence and the greater your ability to lead the wider the circle of your influence became. Influence my people to think differently, awakening the dormant ability of my children. To take a lesson from history and never again commit the same mistakes, to sustain positive attitudes of African and avoid traditional harmful practices, to change unproductively, erase the tendency of dependency and opportunistic behaviors. Maintain the strong and worth work culture.

Influencing my people to wear a very balanced an eye glass to see each other humanely no matter how different their backgrounds is.

Language, color, tribe and race do not matter at the face of love. Influence my children to love one another; my dream is influencing them to cut down the roots of their ignorance, to treat one another equally and fairly.

A human being is a very honorable creature ever created in this world. Build well structured democratic institutions. Influence to set laws and orders. Create conducive environments to meet my people's needs and wants. Influence them to conduct timely and free and fair elections. Enhance independent judiciary institutions and civil societies and create great play grounds for free press development in my land. Influence to struggle against negative attitudes. Against primitive norms ways of thinking and eliminate intolerance. And Influence them to think intolerance by itself is a violation. Influence is the ability to get a person to do something willingly because you want it done.

Influence is different than traditional ways. When one person's opinion overrides the mind-set of the other individual and other individual or group's thinking moves in the desired direction. Influence for me is an ability of being able to direct the thoughts of people in the direction you want them to think. Influence is the ability to alter the thinking patterns of others. The change in thinking pattern may lead to a change in actions/perceptions.

A form of persuasion to affect cognitive and behavioral shifts, over time may Impact others' attitudes, with a desired outcome that corresponds with your interests. It can be tangent or non-tangent.

Influence is the ability to generate unquestioned trust from others. Influence is having an effect, intentional or unintentional on those around you. To influence is to have impact in one way or another affecting another's thoughts, decisions or actions through one's own conscious or unconscious Behavior. Influence is the essence of leadership. It is invisible power. Influence is wide and limitless. It is changing someone's behavior. Making an impact in a situation where you ordinarily wouldn't have much control, it is a way of doing something, rather than sitting back and deciding that there is nothing you can do.

If influence is to effect someone else's or groups thoughts, feelings and behavior such that they conform to your end goal for better or worse. I think it can be positive or negative? Can't it be?

Oh yes it can be positive or negative. If one changes someone thoughts in to something bad, your influence would lead to undesirable outcomes. And its consequence will be disastrous. Still influence has power to do whether useful or harmful things. If you influence others to do something good, the consequence is free from unwanted results. What matter is for what purpose you want to influence someone? In fact, it can be to bless or to curse? Bear in mind affecting someone's thought and behaviors can be for both negative and positive.

Beyond your purpose and intensions, actually your methods and tactics of influences will determine the impact of the influence. It can be intentional or unintentional effect on those around you. You know the power to affect others, seen only in its effect without exertion of force or formal authority.

If we look at the archaic definition: the supposed flowing of an ethereal power or fluid from the stars, thought to have a magical effect on the actions and character of people. While Influence may seem to be magical, like all good magic it requires a lot of skill and practice. When done artfully, it looks effortless.

Therefore, if one quest to save me being Salt of the Earth, then shall became highly influential person. Influential people with influence power understands which methods for what and knows the influence tactics' and methods especially those methods that blesses my people and rise up in unity and one heart to save me and lift my spirit up and compensate me to the rest of my entire life as I was meant to live.

CHAPTER THREE

If influencing others has ways, what could be influencing methods and tactics so far?

How Salt of the Earth communicates with my people has a huge impact on my victory. Your base of power determines what form of influence tactic you would be able to use, in order to grab the attention of others. Some leader with coercive power might gravitate towards assertiveness and forcefulness, leaders with referent power might gravitate towards integration, and someone with expert power might try rationality. You have probably noticed throughout your career that, you must adapt your communication approach to different individuals to help persuade or influence them. The use of influence tactics is also dependent upon whom you are just trying to influence. One may respond to a direct approach, while another respond better to humour, so joking with them may get them on board. There is no right or wrong way to influence people; you simply have to discover the best method in individual situations to achieve a positive result. But when it comes to Organizational and state matter one should have carefully study the best methods and tactics of influence. It's not as simple as individual situations.

Listening to those around us will help us identify the best approach to use. When speaking to them, feedback the same approach they use to influence or persuade others. When it comes to leadership one need to know and understand the effective methods and tactics to acquire influence power. Power has the potential to influence others, but only if it is being used in the right manner. Influence is what drives one's senses to do what otherwise may not be possible. It is to affect someone else's or a group's thought, feeling, and behavior, such that they conform to your end goal for better or worse. The act of influencing can be open and direct, or subtle and indirect or subconscious. Influence is the art of facilitating new personal, group, or universal meaning through different tactics and methods. One can get power over others through various means. The influence power might be invisible power .Your overall success in your call of soul or life, will depend on your ability to influence people in a positive way to achieve your goal. Explore your influence style and strategy and learn how to achieve better result by adapting your style to the preferred method of my African children.

Mama, you told me if one wants to be salt of the earth or any leader in every aspects of life in general, one need to know the effective ways mention some please?

The process of influencing others may contain many cause, and contents. There are various methods to influence others. The methods could be the positive or negative one. As their cause differs, they assert their prone and cons. Got impact according to your method chosen. But if you insist to tell you; I will tell you some common tactics and methods which, had been in use by many leaders intention in my land in many aspects of life. Influence can be with people, things or events. Strength and effectiveness of influence can vary. The process that, leaders use to influence someone can take a variety of forms. An important reason for choosing a specific influence tactic may depend on, what the leader wishes to accomplish. Influence is a force, one person exert on someone else to induce a change, including changes in behavior, opinion, attitude, goal, need and value. Also, it is the ability to affect the behavior of others in a particular direction. To influence others, a leader use strategy or tactics, actual behaviors, designed to change another person's attitude, belief, value or action. Leaders tend to use different tactics and have somewhat different objectives depending on the direction of the influence. For instance, this typically can be seen when a leader attempt to influence someone above them or below them. Influence is changing someone's behavior. Making an impact in a situation where you ordinarily you wouldn't have much control. It is a way of doing something, rather than sit back and deciding that, there is nothing you can do. To make an impact in a situation where one ordinarily would not have much control, use many ways to make others do what one want them to do. Let me tell you the common methods which, one can influence others through …

Manipulation,

Negotiation,

Persuasion,

Teaching,

Inspiration

Exchange,

Positional,

Consultation,

Collaboration,

Power,

Respect,

PERSUATION

The power of persuasion used, to influence another's thoughts or actions. It can be someone's presence, character, attitude, that can affect someone and cause a change in another person's way of thinking or action. The leader use logical arguments and factual evidence to show that, a request or proposal is feasible and relevant for important task objectives. Rational persuasion involves an effort to explain why a request or proposed activity, vision, goal dream and things to do in the best interest of my betterment. Persuasion is Important for attaining shared objectives. The tactic often includes Subjective opinions that cannot be verified. The effectiveness of such information in influencing followers or any target attitude requires leader's credibility.

If the followers perceive that, the leader is exaggerating benefits or providing biased forecast, then the influence attempt is unlikely to be effective. Thus, rational persuasion is easier to use and more likely to be effective when followers trust the leader. It uses logical arguments and factual evidence to persuade others that, a proposal or request is workable and likely to result in mission or duty or task objective. Logical persuasions use logic or evidence to explain or justify a position and rely on knowledge or expertise to present factual reasons, supported by charts, graphs, and data as proof.

Some of my leaders use the existing reality in my land as a proof to persuade others for my success. Leaders need to work through the issue carefully and ensure their case is well planned and supported. Explain why you are making your request and the proposed course of action then ensure that evidence is provided to support your conclusion. What could be the reason for Salt of the Earth explain or justify to the people to go along with him? Simple one shall show my children who truly they are, what they supposed to be and how they are doing. If their present situations continue as is, what will come after? Leaders make people picture their live in different perspective and convince them to follow the best way to do things right and do the right thing. If they don't, then again show its consequences. Actually it can be both the positive and the negative. Then make effort to explain the mere fact and truth alive, and do their best to convince them positively.

Yes we are poor. Yes we are behind the present world and being tail always. This method is reasonable. If the leader use rational persuasion and can buy their heart, not win over their brain. It is decisive. The art of persuasion is a basic art of leadership. This method depends on the ability of leader's persuasion capacity. Leaders have the capacity to speak persuasively and inherit the power of words to win people heart.

TEACHING

This method of influence laid its foundation in the course of teaching. To teach is to craft the people as you want. It is leading through teaching. Leaders who lead its people through teaching believe; - "Knowledge is necessary for the people to change their shame in to glory" That is it. Whereas, teaching, could be positive or negative. It depends on what you teach the people. Even the European came to me at the mask of teaching and civilizing. What you teach determine how much you are going to be productive. If leaders use this method, before acting shall ask, what do they really want to do? Before teaching my people out of the blue, you need to understand what you want. Before asking people to have some characters that you wanted, ask yourself what do you have first? As a leader, you attract who you are, not who you want. It is very necessary to know what to influence. Because we don't attract who we want, we attract who we are. Salt of the earth shall be a very good teacher of all the time. Where are my teachers, elites? Are they paying me back or stand against with my enemies? Who forced the great teachers of mine to leave me alone and go away? I am tired of brain drain.

Leader shall have knowledge and teaching power to lead its

people through teaching. Whilst leaders have special information or expertise that, the people values, people tend to follow one who value them and their value. True leaders respect people's value. This type of power can come from extensive background and education or an area where an individual display extremely proficient skills. It comes through applying knowledge effectively. Teaching power can be very beneficial to any Salt of the Earth. Of all the base of power, expertise is most consistently associated with assistant effectiveness. To get things done require the use of power. Accomplishing modernization and change threaten the status quo. Thus, innovation and change are political activities, because implementations require political will, expertise and the use of power. Both Jesus and Mohamed sought to lead by examples. Leaders that use teaching method to lead are those who are actually exemplary and wise in practical life. You shall make my children follow you in your extraordinary teaching by examples and became Salt of the Earth.

Salt of the Earth has always the capacity to see beyond one natural eyes; it is a picture of purpose. Of course, the world and my people have a picture of my bad image. Salt of the Earth strive to build my image positively. Make all the people knowledgeable. True son of Africa die trying to make, apply and implement their knowledge effectively through teaching. And then, my land shall be flourishing with African wisdom. By the way as far as my knowledge is concerned, wisdom means the capacity to apply knowledge effectively. In my land this tactic may give each of my children the ability to see each other's situations in positive way. Through teaching one can influence my people. So that, negative attitude shall be replace by positive attitude. Salt of the earth has enormous interest of teaching others and has people skill. These are the ability to draw people to one and help them develop their gifts and characters. Leaders have integrity with people and consistency in their words and actions. They live what they teach, are practical. They are change agents who are truly changed and change others via teaching to satisfy their interests.

NEGOTIATION

My future overall success in life will depend on my African leaders' ability to influence people in a positive way to achieve Africans dream. Negotiation in present world is considered to be the score card of politicians. Do my children negotiating for or against me? What does Africans give and take?

Most of the negotiation that took place in my land results confrontation. But negotiation needs not to be confrontational. True leaders know how to negotiate successfully to settle and secure the interests of African people. They adopt a negotiation mind set; focus on their own interests and others. Craft a curious attitude and avoid self-limiting assumptions. If any Africans need to be salt of the earth and use negotiation as one of the influencing method, one do not became emotional and try to win at all costs. Leaders have to understand the other person point of view. And that is why negotiation need not be characterized by negative feelings or angry behaviour. Leaders need to understand the process of negotiation. Because it increases our chance that the outcome of our negotiation to be more positive for both parties.

Negotiation method is neither negative nor positive way of influencing. Somewhat neutral form of influencing tactic is.

Negotiation is alliance building. It is the process by which two or more parties with different needs and goals work to find a mutually acceptable solution to an issue. Because negotiation is an inter-personal process, each negotiating situation is different, and influenced by each party's skills, attitude and style. My children used to negotiate with others and tried to win the contest of wills. As a result, they came up with more difference, dispute and misunderstanding. But it has to be a mutual discussion with the aim of resolving a difference of opinion or dispute.

Negotiation ought to be getting group together to accomplish a common goal, this could not be completed by another person. It is creating a network of supporters and build consensus. Thus, African leaders first must be highly influential person with amazing bargain quality. Or else first get one or more influential or highly-visible person on board, and then others will be more likely to join the group. True leaders negotiate, not win at all costs or to loss but to come up with a win- win solution for me.

EXCHANGE

Exchange is moderate ways of influencing tactic. It is commonly used in many form of leadership. Makes explicit or implicit a promise that others will receive rewards or tangible benefits if they comply with a request or reminds others of a favor that should be reciprocated. In Exchange the leader offers something the people wants, or offers to reciprocate at a later time, if the people will do what the leader requests.

This method gives something of value to influence an individual in return for what you want. Negotiate, bargain, exchange favours, create a win-win situation and comprise. You need to find out what the people needs, values and interests are, and then plan an exchange that will satisfy the people. Think "win-win" and seek comprise, if the person can't grant your request. True leaders avoid having hidden agendas because exchanging is built on trust. A leader shall have trust. Most exchange tactics involve explicit offers to provide a reward if the followers does what the leaders wants.

Proactive exchange tactic in a good relationship contain little need for the leader to offer specific rewards when asking others to carry out a task.

An explicit exchange agreement is more appropriate for dealing with a lateral peer or someone who is not a member of the same background (Nation). In a high relationship between leader and followers, the leader will be trusted to reward the efforts of the followers in a way that is appropriate and equitable. Mostly leaders in my land promise to exchange, promise to commit win- win but ends win- loss. Watch out, what you are exchanging on behalf of me.

INSPIRATION

Inspiration is high level of influencing method. This method makes an emotional request or proposal that arouses enthusiasm by appealing to other's values and ideals, or by increasing their confidence that they can succeed. I quest true African leaders who seeks to arouse my people's emotions to gain commitment for their life betterment and advancement. Salt of the earth need to have passion and shall make my people passionate about life. Passion is the juice for living. For my people life is stiff work. In regard to their jobs, spouses, education or importantly personal development, they feel hard.

Life became tedious work. They have no motivation. Nothing is new. Stay stuck and unmotivated. Africans remain comfortable in daily routines, live in comfort zone. They are obsessed with their past and it in return shadows the present life. Life doesn't count if one misuses the present thinking about the past. This must be changed. So here it come the need to inspire my people to lead change. Unless otherwise Africans have great inspiration towards everything at hand, for sure we will be burdens of others. For how long we say "who cares" if not Africans then who shall care?

Salt of the earth has deep motivation and passion to motivate others. Yes true leaders do not require outside stimuli in order to take actions. They are self motivated. What on earth Africans life seems impossible to change; True leader makes people passionate towards change.

Passion is the driving force for salt of the earth. So, they shall motivate and inspire my children. Any African who dare t be salt of the earth and choose inspiration method to influence my people towards a common cause will achieve visible result. Inspirational method involves attempts to link a proposed activity or change to values and Ideals. One type of inspirational appeal is to communicate a vision of an exciting achievement or a better future. This type of tactic is often used by transformational and charismatic leaders to gain support for new initiatives and major changes. In a strong inspirational power, the leader's high level of trust may make my people more receptive to leader appeals, which involve sacrifices and risk of failure. True leaders have initiatives. They are self starters. They don't need outside urging to do something, they initiate and inspire others. They inspire others not only being great motivational speakers but also they became man of exemplary character.

A true leader who's, positive actions and life becomes a people magnet, and make peoples rally around him. Inspire people to behave in a certain way by setting an example,

Lead by doing and demonstrate the right way to African civilization. They Coach, mentor, assess performance and give feedback. The leaders treat people with respect, empathy, and consideration. Show a positive attitude and provide encouragement, share knowledge and experiences. Practice what they preach – otherwise they may damage their reputation. If my children intend to use inspirational influencing methods to be salt of the earth, they shall show enthusiasm, commitment, dedication and passion. True leader speak in terms of achievement, quality or other desired values. They must share and appeal to their higher values, e.g. loyalty, participation in a cause, or being part of a winning life. You need to build trust and a common ground. If only for your own values do not align with the people, you will not succeed. Leaders inspire to comfort others. Inspiration is the capacity to mobilize, activate, motivate, stimulate and line my children by your side. Salt of the earth's own character and make Africans participate and take part of a change of African priorities. Encourage and inspire my people to keep moving beyond self-sufficiency. Inspiration is the key to aspiration. Earn it. Inspiration is the heart of true leadership.

CONSULTATION

Most of my people are spectaculars of the undertaking developmental endeavours'. Never ask and never been asked to. It seems only few are privileged to do whatever they want to do in my land without consultation of the mass. People deserved to have a say, need to be consulted in everything. African people do not count in the face of vampire leaders. It is tragic. Leaders are parts of their people. And promise to them to serve selflessly with compassion and immediately forgets their people and pretends to work for them. Leadership without the involvement of the mass, never last. True leader leads by consultation.

Consultation is one of the high influencing methods. Consultation seeks others' participation in making a decision or planning, how to implement a new idea, proposed policy, strategy or change. Leader asks the people to suggest improvements or help Plan a proposed activity or change for which the people's support is desired. It appeals to the person's expertise, ask for input, look into for feedback, collaborate and invite the people to participate or become involved. If any Africans dare to be salt of the earth, then shall lead my people through consultation. You need to prepare your proposal and state it in broad terms to allow a lot of latitude when getting a response. Identify issues and assumptions and state exactly what you need. Listen to the people's response and ask open-ended questions. Be genuine Appealing to Friendship - rely on friendships, loyalty, or past relationships to get what you want. Ask for favours, tell them that you need their help or are counting on their support and let them know that they can count on you. You need to recognize and acknowledge any inconvenience your request may cause. Consider doing something for them first. State how important their co-operation is and how much you're counting on their support. Be willing to give back, who works for the best interest of my people shall not refrain in their involvement. If you say I work for the people interest, you shall know the true needs and wants of the people. You can't despise people.

Don't be shallow, stuck in your own, and party interest. Any party that works against my people is not my heart desire. No matter how poor and how illiterate they are, whatsoever my people's attitudes are, Wherever they live, No matter how ignorant my elites are, they are my great assets. Consult them. Do not plan for them without them. You cannot clap by a single hand. People are resources. Create belongingness and share your vision for me within my people. By then,

TWO HANDS MAKES LIGHT WORK!

My children are my great asset.

POSITIONAL

In life, one-way or another you may hold position, or title. Unless my people are convinced about what you are about, they may not be ok with you. You may have big titles or may hold high status in your society. My people might cautiously comply with what you have to say without necessarily following you. Salt of the earth lets the people know what he is all about and convince them to rally around him as a people magnet. As I told you if my people are not convinced about what you are about, they may not be ok with you. Leaders who use position or titles methods to influence others always focus on legitimatizing. They show people that what they want is consistent with policy and procedures and refer to requests or directives of management.

Positional influencing method refers to policies and procedures as a basis for any decision. What if my people are not comfortable with the policy and procedures, which positional leaders craft and endorse without the will and say of the people? Leadership is winning peoples heart to follow you for a common cause. Remember your position do not perform what you do. Leaders with this method cite higher management when making their request and speak authoritatively and confidently. This Behavior seeks to persuade others that the request is something they should comply with given their situation or position. They do not try to convince others to do things. A leader may have a position that may be in control .in that position one may have authority, but real leadership is more than having authority. True leadership is more than having the technical training and following the proper procedure. Any African can play a leadership role without holding certain leadership positions and titles. Remember not everyone who holds a certain position is necessarily a leader. I had quite lots of leaders with high positions and tittles in my land ever. But they never could win my peoples heart. Salt of the earth is not about a title rather it is selfless service, which one carry out and proves in daily life. As long as there is no positive influence there is no leadership that fits my hearth desire. Position tactic is low means to influence others. For the leader that uses position to influence others, their security is based on title, not talent. One cannot be more secure and confident unless people follow him gladly and confidently. You see, I quest a leader who is full of acting service that one offer continuously and diligently with and without tittles. A leader who stays at this level gets in to territorial rights, protocol, tradition and organizational charts. These things are not negative unless they became the basis for authority and influence, but they are poor substitutes for leadership skills. Positional method involves efforts to demonstrate that a request is legitimate and the leader has the authority to make it. But if we look at issues related to; who drafts the laws, procedures and proclamations for my land? Who endorses? Did they buy the will of the people to draft and endorse to take actions, or forced my people to obey whatever the leaders' wishes? What will this tactics will bring? Its consequences shall be resentment, dissatisfaction and envy. To become salt of the earth is to go beyond position and tittles. I have witnessed most of my leaders with positional influence, were overthrown, put out of office and trampled underfoot. People normally follow leaders, if they are truly influenced and convinced wherever they lead them. But positional tactics often gained by appointment, not by ability. Practically in my land you earn authority or position through family ties, bribes, fraud and being loyal to and became particular party member. If one obtains position by merits, that's good. But position may not allow you to make people follow you in the extra mile you want to take them. So, people will not follow positional leaders beyond their stated authority. You need to impress my children within and out together for my African dream to be fulfilled. Have positive influence power; to make my African dreams comes true.

COOLABORATION

For most of my leaders, truly hearing a deferent perspective is not easy, when the roar of their own thoughts drown everything else out. They hear only what they say, not others. Straggle to assert their own set of principles, values, approaches and solutions, which can easily, became rigid. Salt of the Earth do not see himself as right and others simply wrong, at best, inadequate. We need a team; partners and aliens, when we need something better done.

True leaders do not say; - "we need to find a solution and I have got it" rather, turn my people in to collaborator. Through collaboration one can make difference.

Collaboration Includes aspects of supportive leadership such as offering to help my people carry out a requested task or to provide adequate resources to do the task. Correlated positively with supportive leadership Therefore, it is likely that collaboration increases the positive effect of people toward the Leader. Moreover, the leader is more likely to ask them to perform difficult tasks for which it is appropriate to provide additional resources and assistance. Salt of the earth are anticipated to create public mobilization, make my children as pillars, to build Africa. Collaboration with others create positive outcome.

RESPECT

Influencing others through respect has high level of effectiveness. People follow because of who you are and what you represent. Respect offers you referent power; it exists when the power holder is well liked by others. In this sense, charismatic leaders will have referent power. This type power is interesting in the way that the followers are easily influenced, due to the genuine respect they hold for their leader. The leader who is popular and well liked is more apt to gain favorable response without the use of power or coercion. Networking in the workplace can be extremely beneficial for this type of leaders, since one can form a basis, for calling in favors in time of need. Influencing through respect method uses Socializing; Salt of the Earth do not organize a network patronage to get the job done rather, behave in a warm and friendly manner in order to influence unfamiliar person or the people to cooperate. To be salt of the earth is to be friendly.

If you became interested, build a relationship or rapport, and need to introduce yourself in a friendly and open manner, listen actively and ask questions and show interest by discussing things you have in common. If my children dare to use this method, then shall have personal warmth. It's the leader's manner and attitude that drive people towards a common goal. The law of respect is people naturally follow leaders who are stronger than themselves. If people do not have trust in you as a leader, they neither respect nor follow you. Win my Africans heart with a genuine and warm respect.

FORCE, PRESSURE

The use of power or force is one of the common influencing tactic and method. Muscle was one alternative or means used by many of my leaders. Be it the former or the present leaders of mine pretend to be democrats but in reality they prefer to show their muscle for everything. Pressure tactic is one of the worst and most practiced method.

Leaders who use force to influence are not certain about themselves. Either they got the ability to lead or not. They came through power by overthrown one and lead by coercive power. They came to secure peace and justice through trickery election and eat their word. They exert pressure to do whatever they intend to do. They don't consult or convince my people or participate them, rather they want the people only to conform their decision is the best for the people.

They use power in order to make my people act or believe for their own behalf; it is a set of cynical beliefs about human nature, morality, and the permissibility of using various tactics to achieve one's ends. The force method includes demands, threats or intimidation to convince others to obey with a request or to support a proposal. Leaders with coercive power do not care for public interest. Whichever the interest of the people, and wants them to think or do in the direction of them. Whatsoever the people wants and needs are, dictators want my people to decorate their ideology. No matter how important the public opinion is, their actions, decisions and thoughts are, they simply left you no choice in the decision. They are dictators'. They dictate your life as they wish .use their power against you. Coercive power essentially is dishonest and unethical tactic. It is ruthlessly manipulative. In fact, there is always power in leadership. However salt of the earth turn that power in to selfless service for my advancement. Of course, salt of the earth have power. Their leadership power is to use for my people; not against them. The purposes of leadership power are enabling and serving others; it is not only controlling and ruling. But if you look at my dreadful leaders, they use power to control my people to do what they told them to do. Only in the interest of the leader or the party which the leader belongs comes first. That is it.

In coercive power justice is a loaded gun, and good governance is people who are under in control of well structured militant's hand. I am sick of my leaders with coercive power. Though I am their mother, am ashamed of them. Most pressure tactics are based on coercive power, and extensive use of such tactics can be expected to elicit resentment and negative effect in Africans people.

This effect is reason to expect negative relationships among my leaders and my people. Even doesn't fit my heart desire. Pressure tactic can undermine personal trust and traits positive effect. Leaders must immediately avoid using force to influence my people. Still, my leaders use demands, threats, frequent checking, or persistent Reminders to influence my people to do something. Dear my dictator children open your eyes; - beware of the value of every single creature in my land. Stop enjoying your sisters and brothers suffering. Have mercy, may be one day you will be given mercy, of course, you will seek it soon. Believe me everything changes except the word change itself. You shall stop sucking blood, don't intoxicate yourself with Africans blood.

MANIPULATION

Manipulation implies intent to fool or trick somebody into doing, believing, or buying something that leaves them harmed in some way. We view manipulators as schemers. Out to get what they want using whatever means possible.

Manipulators selfishly pursue their own agenda, trying to control the people.   They do not make an effort to positively influence rather; manage and utilize my people skillfully to control indirectly, play upon by artful, unfair, or insidious means especially to their own advantages, against my people interest. They conceal a desire to move my people to their point of view in a way that will only benefit them. In addition, to influence through manipulation means shrewdly or deviously tamper with or falsify for personal gain. It is to change by artful or unfair means so as to serve one's purpose. I prefer my leaders to have positive Influence that is long lasting. However manipulation is a short term, which will always come out. Getting my people to do you a favor you believe that they won't want to do is leading through manipulation. Manipulation is making others to do what you want through fear. Using guilt or emotional blackmails, is not my heart desire. To lead by manipulation tactic may accomplish what you want, but it does not make you true leader. It is inability to win over people's heart. By the way son, As soon as the people recognize or feel manipulated, they start to regret about it. If their intention were uncovered, the discovery would cause the other person to be less receptive to their idea. In the selfless service of salt of the earth, all information provided is accurate and shared openly to win over people's heart. But in manipulation, Information is withheld or distorted to trick or deceive. The Reason behind the intention to persuade another person is hidden. Truthfulness and accuracy of provided information is not there. Transparency of the process is not given clearly. Therefore, Manipulation method benefits the manipulators only, and affect, or impact my children. To lead my people via manipulation to something lead to eventual regret. It is unethical. Leaders who dare to influence my people through manipulation method do not count worth for me, rather lags me behind to live before my age. Positive Influence lasts long and follows ethical manner. Plus I expect my leaders to choose the positive and effective influencing methods to serve me for the hope I incepted now a days.

Oh mama, I believe you took the necessary time to tell me the common methods of influencing others, how can we conclude these issue so far?

People whoever they are, no matter their social status, or whatever their current conditions, whichever they are members of, who aim for a positive outcome need to diagnose the situation. As well as, determine if a hard/push tactic or a soft/pull tactic would be appropriate to be a servant leader. A leadership in every aspects of life must think which methods are best for what before leading and acting. Mastering the art of influence is a key leadership component. Successful leaders understand what influence tactic works best for the situation and the person or group. If the desired results aren't obtained, perhaps the wrong tactic is being used. Effective leadership and influence has available a wide array of tactics.

Often, potential leaders use the same tactic over and over, getting few results, because the tactic was applied inappropriately. If ideas are to be accepted towards a given change, leaders must learn the art of influence. Therefore, any leadership that restricts, denies inhibits, limits suppresses, oppresses, obstructs or frustrates others forcefully is not leadership at all. It is blood sucking mission. Mastering the art of influence is a key leadership component. Having in mind this, according to my quest and wish, every Salt of the Earth shall master positive art of influence. Mastering the art of influence is a key leadership component. Successful leaders skillfully use different tactics under different situations to change behavior, opinion, attitude, goal, need and value of my people, at large to bless not to curse.

In regard s to the sex or gender situation, in your vacancy both male and female salt of the earth are indicated .can a woman lead, could she be salt of the earth for real?
Well before, I come up with a direct answer whether a woman can be a leader or not, let me ask you a question?
What were you calling me, mama Africa or father Africa? Why others and you call me so far?

I don't know why others say so. I might be mistaken but, I call you Mama because I want to show some sort of respect for you. You see son, woman deserves respect. Looking for respect more than recognition, the most successful women leaders don't seek to become the star of the show but, they enable others to create a great show. In other words, being in the spotlight is not what drive woman but, it's the ability to influence positive outcomes with maximum impact. There is a Malawian proverb that says; - "He who thinks he is leading and has no one following him is only taking a walk." That's true.

Leaders who can't inspire others to go with him lack the true essence of leadership. One cannot be a leader without followers. Leadership is a trusted privilege given by followers. And woman are best of it .they possess the power of influence to do so. That is why being in the spotlight is not what drives them – rather it's the ability to influence positive outcome with maximum impact.

Women don't rely on favors; they earn respect and truly believe they can influence their own advancement by serving others. Great leaders never desire to lead but to serve. One thing is certain: these women leaders understand survival, renewal and reinvention. They have grit and are not afraid to fight for what they believe in or an opportunity to achieve something of significance.

They believe in what they stand for, but that doesn't mean they won't put their ideas and ideals to the test.   The eagle tests before it trusts. For woman, doing more with less is simply a matter of knowing how to strategically activate those around them. Leadership is the ability to lead others by influence.

Everyone has the capacity to become a leader. We are created to rule, govern and influence the earth. Of course, everyone has the capacity and potential to become Salt of the Earth. However son, what makes one a leader? What are distinct characteristics that are common to leadership? It's some basic ingredients, characters and skills makes one my leader and distinct from others.

Woman possesses natural leadership skills. A woman's instincts and emotional intelligence can be off the chart. They function differently; their leadership function is different than man. They were never created to be dominated. Both man and female created to influence the earth. It's not secret where they come from: the leadership character that women leaders naturally possess are the most undervalued. Women are more likely than men to possess the leadership qualities that are associated with success. That is, women are more transformational than men - they care more about developing their followers, they listen to them and stimulate them to think "outside the box". They are more inspirational, are more ethical. Inspiration is the key to true leadership. The source of inspiration is passion. Woman has the ability to communicate their passion to others. They are passionate. While women in general were historically viewed and stereotyped as emotional leaders by men, I believe they are just passionate explorers in pursuit of excellence. When women leaders are not satisfied with the status quo, they will make things better. These women leaders get things done and avoid procrastination. They enjoy order and stability and a genuine sense of control. Many women have learned not to depend upon others for their advancement and thus have a tendency to be too independent. A woman's independent nature is her way of finding her focus and dialing up her pursuits. At this critical time as a mother of Africa, I urge urgently to have independent minded leader, because the ultimate goal of leadership is independence. When these women leaders are locked into what they are searching for – move out of the way. Their passionate pursuits allow them to become potent pioneers of new possibilities.

When confronted with a challenge, the women look for the opportunity within. They see the glass as half-full rather than half-empty.

They push the boundaries, when faced with adverse circumstances; they learn all they can from it. Optimism is their mindset, they see opportunity in everything. Passion comes from purpose. And women are purposeful and meaningful. Many women leaders enjoy inspiring others to achieve. They know what it's like to be the underdog and work hard not to disappoint themselves and others.

Women leaders in particular often have high standards and their attention to detail makes it difficult for others to cut corner or abuse any special privileges. Women leaders with a nurturing nature are good listeners and excellent networkers or connecters. They enjoy creating ecosystems and support a collaborative leadership style that meld the thinking and ideas of others; this is what multiplies the size of an opportunity and/or its speed in execution in order to create a larger sphere of influence and overall impact. Women who don't have to be right all the time make good consensus builders and will more likely enjoy participating in a team environment. They are good negotiators, Team builders, suitable to work with others. Woman are consummate team players, also seek to prove their value and self-worth by exceeding performance expectations.

The qualities of my children's character are the measure of their leadership effectiveness.

Women are Strategic; see what often times others don't see. , A woman's lens of skepticism oftentimes forces them to see well beyond the most obvious details before them. They enjoy stretching their perspective to broaden their observations. Many women are not hesitant to peel the onion in order to get to the root of the matter. They Are-risk takers. At times they "play the part" to test the intentions of others and to assure that they are solidly grounded and reliable. Successful women leaders know how to play the game when they have to – and can anticipate the unexpected. They know what cards to play and keenly calculate the timing of each move they make.

They possess great problem solving skills. Women are big believers in team building and the enforcement of mission, goals and values to assure that everyone is on the same page with like intentions. This secures a sense of continuity making it easier for everyone to have each other's back. I wouldn't be surprised to learn a woman leader made the word "organic" or natural. I learned that women who enjoy the ebb and flow of business activity also know that the best things are accomplished when they are done naturally – and unforced. Women leaders enjoy taking charge before circumstances force their hand. They have initiative, are usually the ones to secure the foundational roots of the family and to protect family and cultural traditions from wavering. They provide the leadership within the home and in the workplace to assure that legacies remain strong by means of feed with the right nutrients and ingredients. When things are happening organically, this means that they are functioning within a natural rhythm and speed – that is safer and risk adverse. This is not to say that women are uncomfortable with risk – in fact, will often tackle risk head-on in order to get to the root cause of a problem and to solve for it . Women leaders who don't allow their egos to stand in the way of good business are, in the mindset of getting things done, for the betterment of a healthier whole. - risk taker, knows how to use of resources effectively. "Without enough of the right resources around them they will not risk the outcome. They value time and money. They know the resources they need to get the job done right. They'd rather be patient than foolish. Women understand if one miss use something one will definitely mismanage.

Salt of the earth is innovator and Entrepreneurial. Entrepreneurship is just a way of life for many women. They can be extremely resourceful, connect the dot of opportunity and become expert in developing the relationships they need to get the job done. Many women leaders also see through an entrepreneurial lens to best enable the opportunities before them. They know that to create and sustain momentum requires 100% focus on the objective – and so, they don't enjoy being disrupted by unnecessary noise and distractions. Women can play into the politics of the workplace, and do so if it means adding value to the momentum, they are attempting to create.

This is why women like control, not necessarily to be in charge, but to not lose the rhythm or compromise the momentum they need to accomplish their goals. Woman to be in control, do not want necessarily a title or a position or be in charge to get things done. Relatively exert influence power and that is how they lead and became Salt of the Earth.

So, why do men dominate leadership positions, and why can't women get to the top?

Woman are playing the central role in development drama, and also transmit values to the next generation, their inherited huge leadership capacity encountered multi-faced challenges. Leave alone in my land woman in the world, tend to be poorer than men, are more deprived in health and education and in freedoms in all forms. Due to negative gender stereotypes, gender solidarity, historical, discrimination, religious thoughts, doctrines, etc...woman found themselves limited control over their spouses income, have less access to education, formal sector employment, social security, government employment programs, often paid less for performing similar tasks.

Legislation and social custom often prohibit woman from owning property or signing financial contracts without a husband signature. Have primarily responsibility for child rearing. Tend to spend a significantly higher fraction of income under their control for the benefits of their children than fathers do. These woman challenges generally include work, life balance, parenting, juggling many responsibilities and multi-tasking. Challenges specific to women continue to be a wage gap - women still earn less of what men do for the same job. Discrimination remains present in the workplace; sexual harassment and many more. While men are offered a "free pass.", our image of a leader is "male," and so we more often select or promote men. Men control the hiring and favor men over women. We are simply reluctant to change the status quo. If there were more woman leaders in my land it would be a better place. But woman are surrounded with the biggest challenges. In addition, most of my nations had no a gender-balanced board or management team. .the essence of becoming my salt of the earth is to know and becoming you. Women cannot be man neither man does so. They both function differently at the same time shares common characters and biologically distinct each other. Therefore it's true both can function differently as their very nature.

It can be difficult for a man to understand how women think, act and innovate unless, he has been closely influenced by the women in his life, know women may process things differently and in their own terms. , men who've been influenced by great women understand their capacity and their approach towards leadership. And will understand their decision-making processes.

The dynamics and subtlety of their personality and style, and other special character qualities that women possess, Shall come for front through sustainable women empowerment. Significant emphasis must be given. Women invest in themselves and become knowledge seekers. They are not afraid to ask questions when given a safe platform to express themselves, are also more inspired to adopt new ideas and ideals. Though extremely curious, it's often balanced with a bit of skepticism – after all, they don't want to be fooled or taken advantage of. But woman lack great awareness about themselves. We all should think about their true nature. So that, will understand the power of woman. These women leaders enjoy a good challenge – and seek to find meaning and purpose from each circumstance, they face and opportunity they are given. They like to see and understand the connectivity of thoughts and how they work or why they don't. They want all the facts and figures before making important decisions. And this shall never make them considered poor decision makers. Women need to identify their unique talents, understand what they bring to their work environment to best enable success, and then, make sure that their voice is heard. Speak up, speak out, and contribute. Women may experience difficulty with this in many work environments. So, it's important to find a community within my home land – mentors, role-models, networking groups – who can help navigate through an organization and provide a support system. Throughout the continent and the world as a whole which focused on my children. Significant emphasis must be placed on discovering woman leadership capacities awareness on who truly woman are, and woman empowerment. Be it self-empowerment, self discovery within or out. Besides solving their multifaceted social, economic and political challenges, Women's networking groups, mentoring and development are important to women. But, ultimately, a community that genuinely cares about their women leaders keeps their women. Need to have active policies in place that ensure equal rights for women and have taken active steps to redress that imbalance, became most successful.

But for most, it is up to African woman to fully understand who truly they are and discover the hidden natural leadership ability within. I encourage my leader to give thoughtful attention to creating a gender-neutral environment. To do that, they must first truly understand women in general. Yes of course, a woman can be salt of the earth.

I quest African woman to be prepared and became an effective leader that, saltine my land as my heart desire. Leadership is born out of character and determination. And I know woman are naturally blessed with the necessarily characters. But must be care full not to use your influence power in different direction of my dream. If it is so, their natural influence power became corrupted influence.

What's that all about?

It is all about influence with bad cause and negative outcome with a maximum impact. It is fact that life is all about cause and effects we have seen it in the course of history like that of Delilah, Eve, etc... So long as influence power is not managed and applied with positive attitude and good will, it is inevitable to result curse in my land. My female children should be well aware and careful about it.

Generally speaking, the paradox of your question is part of a wider paradox in modern society on the subject of gender and leadership.

In an era when women have made sweeping strides in educational attainment and workforce participation, relatively few African women have made the journey all the way to the highest levels of political or corporate leadership. Especially those of Africa America women's are at the lead. And I hope there may come more African woman salt of the earth following my quest. Thus I need my women's determination to pay all the necessarily prices of Salt of the Earth.

CHAPTER FOUR

Mama   you mention the salary, as per the price of the current salt of the earth in your continental call what about it?

As soon as you become a leader, you lose the right to think about yourself, instead you start thinking more about the wellbeing of others.   The true nature of leadership is sacrifice.   Those of my children with devilish attitude will never seem to lose their appetite for cruel farce. One shall be aware of the tragic destiny that await him and must be brave to survive it.   Son, let me be clear: leadership is hard, but worth it. The prize is enormous and worthwhile. We are constantly and pleasantly surprised by the ways in which leaders in a myriad of setting bring meaning and high performance to organizations and nations.

Leaders provide purpose, excitement and anticipation.

They live on the edge between uniqueness and a necessary degree of conformity. They make all the difference. However, to make a difference in my entire territory, will inquire you to pay huge price of leadership. Beyond the leadership prize you get.

Whichever of my child who is eager to be salt of the earth according to my quest and pertain to stand forefront, should be well informed and ready concerning the continual battle of leadership. Leadership Battle contains too much ups and downs. It is not a matter of protocol to be a true leader. Relatively it goes beyond the boast and use of luxurious cars. It goes beyond to owe fancy house and huge salary. The essence of Salt of the earth is not a privilege to do whatever you want, its huge and unique responsibility.

Leadership responsibility makes you to be one step ahead of your followers. The leadership process may put you in hot water and hot pan again and again, yet it will be a privilege when it is given by your followers. Generally, the process of salt of the earth requires you to be baptized of epiphany of misery in your selfless services. As a result, you need to pay the price. Be it low or high. In that case, you can be my servant leader ever.

What makes the price low or high?

Oh! It varies and depends on time and situations but particularly in my land, the price is very high. It costs you a lot. For instance, the price of pan- African movement to the independent Africa costs from personal insolence to the exile.

The existing reality of my land determines the cost of leadership. It depends on the consciousness of my people in every generation. The price of salt of the earth relies on my existing situation and people mind-set towards everything. It also relay on the atmosphere of political climate. The mood of African politics determine African leadership price.

Politics is supposed to be the practice and theory of influencing other people on a civic or individual level. It is How crippled children walk, the mentally ill get care, roads are built, healthcare is provided, children are thought. Thus far most of my children said and entered politics to serve others. Few did much good, and most of them have sinned and fall short of the glory of selfless service.

Politics suppose to provide special opportunities to share compassion with African people who are deprived, starving and powerless. Politics involves what we do together to make our life better, recognizing that sometimes the actual result can be that we make our lives together worse. To be evidence for you, of the 107 African leaders overthrown between 1960 and2003 two-thirds were murdered, jailed or slung in to exile. Up until 1979, 59 African leaders were toppled or assassinated. Only three retired peacefully and not one was vote out of office. No incumbent African leader ever lost an election until1982.

It pits me, its consequences gets high costs when it comes to my land. Here they are; - the common prices of salt of the earth: - Criticism, Opposition, rejection, Loneliness Imperilment, Betrayal, Murder, assassination, unpleasing people etc...

I think it is very important to know the details of every price to be paid on the delivery of salt of the earth service for all your children before they simply pertain to be there for you? Would you take your time to elaborate each one of them?

Yes I love to. It will assist them to make sure before they go through. Let me start with criticism:-

CRITICIZM

Salt of the earth is believed to be a vital decision maker. Decision making is a daily task to do so. Decision is selecting one alternative of the available alternative.

Selecting and passing decision is mandatory for every leader. If two good options available, selecting the better good. If bad, choosing the best evil. No matter how important your decision is, no matter how hard you try to attain your goal on the best interest of my children. One seek it and others question it and will do their best to make your decisions insignificant and of no value. They execute this to you on purpose or innocently. As you became leader, you will be criticized. You will receive infinite unconstructive critics while you stay loyal to your mission. It's obvious you cannot skip from critic, if you stay in the course of serving the people at large. It is a way of leadership. No true leader is exempt. Criticism is the manifestation of jealousy and insecurity. No matter how far the sky is, it very near to those of my children, who sit cross handed and do nothing, but busy to criticize you. Salts of the earth never trill themselves while they face critic. Quite think others have right to criticize them. For a leader, it is the measurement of maturity to be criticized. It Shows how determinant and devoted to its vision. Receiving criticism is an opportunity to build yourself and your stand to me. Wait for it. If you are prepared to be criticized, then, get prepared to be salt of the earth. Those successful people do not have time to criticize you, they are confident that your leadership never let them down and never jealous of you. Be conscious of there is always to be beaten up by the stick and sharp tongue of others. If you are true servant leader, criticism is ahead of you. As a leader, you need to survive sore criticism. Survive an acidic tongue. Criticism is supposed to be the practice of judging the merits and faults of something or someone in a logical or articulate way. As I told you, one quest to save me and one's idea to make me fall. Those who works eight days a week to save me will be disgusted and out of favor by those who never be asleep to see me fall. No matter how blessing your leadership is, they see nothing good in what you do. They may approach you, in a way of highly specific, detailed or very abstract and general. Criticism possibly will appear in the course of verbal or non-verbal, expressed symbolically, or expressed through an action or a way of behaving. Whichever line of attack they approach you, it is to verify that, you are good for nothing in their face.

Does criticism necessarily mean to let one down?

Often to criticize does not necessarily lead "to find fault", but the word is often taken to mean the simple expression of an objection against prejudice, or a disapproval. Often criticism involves active disagreement, but it may only mean "taking sides". It could just be an exploration of the different sides of an issue. Fighting is not necessarily involved.   Criticism is often presented as something unpleasant, but it need not be. It could be friendly criticism, amicably discussed, and some people find great pleasure in criticism "keeping people sharp", but the fear of losing what they have been doing, may be disturbed.

Once you became transformational leader Your newly effort will disturb and prevent their bad doings. As a result, they never criticize you to make you sharp on your carrier. They shall never offer you constructive criticism. Using unpleasant criticism, drive you to say; - "OK I QUIT OR OK AM OUT! " Mostly dangerous people are often people who build their lives by destroy others. Whoever they are those who criticize you. Don't bother yourself.   Pick wisdom and direction out from every criticism without infected.   There is nothing like selfless service without criticism. Do not let whichever criticism to wound your heart. No matter how big they attempt to magnify your weakness.

Remember salt of the earth is not a fatalist. Let off and move on. I have experienced new wave of criticism, as many of you know. There is nothing like leadership without accusation. Beside criticisms, you may be opposed and rejected.

OPOSITION AND REJECTION

Change is all the agenda, for any salt of the earth, to spread betterment and development of my people. Leaders exemplify sound effects. They are catalyst of change. Change leads you to the place you haven't been before. It revolutionizes current state of affairs. It prefers the modern way than habitual ways and Move you from the common to uncommon. Yes I believe in change. Change can shift my children and me from the epoch of uncivilized land to environmentally conducive, fertile land.

Change is good, As well is very dangerous.

How Mama?

Change makes you come out of your comfort zone. If you see my people, they love change; they are enthusiastic about change.

Everyone love change but fearful or unwilling to be changed. That's the problem you are going to face as leader. Since it is up to you to spark change and transmit peoples live. If you desire to change and be changed my people, primary their comfort zone shall come to an end. If not, While you maintain them, they split you up. While you bless them, they curse you. It is common, where there is change; resistance to change is in place. No matter how enthusiastic my children are about change and how happy they are for the new life you determined to offer them, they may Reject and oppose you because you are going to change them. Though people need change, normally resist to be changed.

Mama, I wonder to know if one need change, why refuse to go along with it in any way?

In actual fact, the opposition and rejection ahead of you, depends on how you present the new plan. As I told you, people for many reasons refuse to accept change. They prefer to live with their old problems than your new solutions. Uncertainty about your new idea and fear of losing their past possibly will resist you. Due to the behavior of change and the scar of poor leadership, they passed all the way through and live within could come with stiff opposition to your new idea.

Any African, who wishes to be my servant leader, should be willing to be rejected and misunderstood by all. True leaders affect change, and change by its very nature cause danger and resistance. Accordingly You May be totally rejected and May not be appreciated or recognized. My enemies may possibly hate and reject you, Became your enemies too.

I am driven to live in - realm of darkness, illiteracy and negativity. Understanding my situation you initiate to change me, the gloomy to light, Move my children from illiteracy to the path of literacy, my Negativity to positivity. Subsequently Due to lots of reasons they will pay you rejection and opposition back to, in return to serving them altruistically. You ought to be aware it. Habitually, People prefer to stay with their problems than new solutions.

No one stand upright by itself at first. You need to crawl and try again and again up to the day; you fully found yourself upright position. Any true leader, never does salt of the earth, could get the job done without others. Working with others invites disagreements and misunderstanding, does not necessarily make you much-loved for long. Salt of the earth never stuck or stay sponge with others to be peaceful or feel secured by people all around him. Be courageous to face and survive rejection and opposition, then you be capable to make my life salubrious. Never let rejection and opposition by others obstruct you from the road to rediscover an African mood of civilizations. You need to glimpse my renaissance happen in near future. I understand how complicated the prices it takes to rediscover me. From now, every step of salt of the earth's leadership encounters real antagonism. It is part of noble service. Look forward to it, never be sidetracked or deterred by others opposition or rejection. What about loneliness?

Loneliness…

You know what it is son; it needs to be out front there all the time, when it comes to be salt of the earth. True Leaders appear and stand first before followers. To be frontage of the crowd, it is up to salt of the earth to pass decisive decisions that directly or indirectly affects my people. Many decisions are left to leaders. Leaders face the challenge while others ran away. Such a life of full of decision is a road to loneliness. Salt of the earth are visionary. They always finish first in mind and starts doing it then do at a time. You got to expect loneliness in leadership. It is must to live within one's own internal success. As well, face very kind of challenge. Salt of the Earth never live peacefully, its fact, people never stand and remain by your side all the time. Even those whom you trust much may give you their back. In leadership there may not be a permanent place to stay. Always, remember the true place to stay or live for Salt of the Earth is in people's heart. Relay on conciseness drive you to loneliness.

Salt of the Earth is living for others, safeguarding others, stands for people's interest and right. So the repayment for your unselfish and noble leadership is loneliness. However living for others in leadership is the true essence of life. The journey kept back you alone. The walk to be the light of the world is loneliness. Salt of the earth thinks: - "if my life doesn't value others, life is valueless." , Leaders life is full of ups and downs. At time of difficulty, true leader need to face the world alone, advisors, colleges and followers, may not face the big gunfire of public opinion. Here came to my mind some great words from William Shakespeare: -

"Uneasy lies the head that wears a crown" Healing the wounded mind, blighting the lost hearts and saving the walking dead, are the actions of Salt of the Earth. The journey of Leadership is enormous. Yes. The saviors walk alone all along. Its price is loneliness. The price of faithfulness to conscience is loneliness. The price of adherence to principle is loneliness. I think it is inescapable. The Savior of the world was a man who walked in loneliness.

I do not know of any statement more underlined with the pathos of loneliness than this statement: - "The foxes have holes, and the birds of the air have nests; but the Son of man hath not where to lay his head" Salt of the Earth pay the price of loneliness, those of my true leaders were berated and persecuted and looked down upon. As you became a leader, directly found yourself in a position of loneliness, the loneliness of leadership from which you cannot shrink nor run away and which you must face up to with boldness and courage and ability. You may be fired. You may be told not to come back and forced to give up your blessing service but you keep on. Never give up.

But you are expected t to go out into the entire continent where you are not going to have others like you. You will feel the loneliness of your faith. It is not easy, for instance, to be virtuous when all about you there are those who scoff at virtue. It is not easy to be honest when all about you there are those who are interested only in making resistance.

It is not always easy to be temperate when all about you there are those who make fun of you. It is not easy to be industrious when all about you there are those who do not believe in the value of work. It is not easy to be a man of integrity when all about you there are those who will relinquish principle for expediency. Of course, I would like to say to you here today, my children, if you are ready for my quest for salt of the earth. There is loneliness. Leaders of my heart desire have to live with his conscience.

Leaders have to live with his principles. Leaders have to live with their convictions. Leaders have to live with their testimony. Unless he they does so, they are miserable dreadfully miserable. While there may be thorn, while there may be disappointment, while there may be trouble and travail, heartache and heartbreak, and desperate loneliness, I think that is the leadership price ahead of you. As a servant of my people and the greatest hope of this generation, I invoke upon you every joy as you go forward in your lives to rich and marvelously fruitful experiences, When your voice becomes a lonely voice in the wilderness, you be aware of it. It' is part of the quest. You may be troubled on every side, yet not be distressed; you may be perplexed, but not be despair; Persecuted, but wont forsaken; cast down, but not destroyed.

IMPRISONMENT

Leadership is not easy. While you rise up to saltine my land, people of mine who don't want to see me walk upright or gently, will make you pay lots of the price and suffer you. Made you live where you never think of. They Charge and Sentences you unfairly, for which the things, you never commit. They forge and document against you. Hire untrue witness. Handover you to court, which works all by their side and offer you undesired and unfair punishment. So, imprisonment for Salt of the earth is to be anticipated. You might be bounded in a cell which may be four sided, 20 foot wall with guard and dogs on top. No matter how righteous in your carrier you are, how loyal you are to your vision, courageous to serve the people at large tirelessly, they will put you in prison, even for the rest of your life. Even though, you are limited physically, due to your brothers and sisters unfair just system, they cannot stop your imagination power and control your new thoughts. If you are prepared to pay the price for what you do and don't, you will be remembered in spirit and your legacy shall revitalize. Your thought can not be imprisoned. So you become all alive again. Your endurance to remain firm for what you believe, will create remarkable influence on others and able to create countless followers. To be ready for imprisonments, will pave the way to be Salt of the Earth. Those of my children who, cannot see what you envision for me, will accuse you with treason against me. Pointe their fingers at you, for disobeying the ruling authority that works for its party interest only. They blame you, for criticizing their sovereign, through your loyal service to bless my land. Because of your courageous and extraordinary achievement, they act against you .as you work strong to change the corrupted political system, and try your best to bring their poor leadership to end. You will be imprisoned even killed for treason against the failed state. As if they are the only appointee of the almighty and as if they are the master race of the land, as if they are the only savior of my land. They torture, demoralize and suffer you, to refrain from your great dream that you wished for me. Such children of mine always are afraid of individuals with new alternative ideas. They pretend to be leaders but, are intolerant of new perspectives. They are like a living jelly fish, when you think you catch them, they slip away through your fingers. Expect the countless traps of African vampire leaders.

BITRIAL, DISLOYALITY.

Leadership is all about trust. My people should trust you and you shall have trust in them, right through your journey to put me on the chair of excellence. When time comes and goes, often those whom you have great confidence and trust in, may stand against you as they were not by your side. Someone who betrays others is commonly a traitor or betrayer. You will be betrayed, in your leadership no matter how small or big it is shall come up to your way. Traitors or betrayers happen all along your journey to be Salt of the Earth. If it seems you have no betrayer, may come at, the eleventh hour. It is common in leadership. Salt of the Earth place trust in people and go on in my land of which they are African. If this trust is betrayed, at its worst, shall never let you suffer psychological betrayal trauma. Betrayal trauma has symptoms similar to post traumatic stress disorder, although the element of amnesia and dissociation is likely to be greater. You have got to survive betrayal, never be horrified by the actions or thoughts of those who betray you. It happens at all time everywhere. Even at your astonishing journey to bring prosperity for my people and me. Due to lots of reasons, your friends, your followers and families whom, you place your trust much, will give you their back someday. Leave alone others but, your own people might betray you. Go over it, and survive betrayal. Your followers might forsake you and flee. Your family may do not go along with you. They may Say to you;-"you don't belong with us", you may be cast out, also put in the dark hole. Whatever happens, whoever betray you, vindicate in the long run.

Betrayal is the breaking or violation of a presumptive contract trust or confidence. It produces moral and psychological conflict within a relationship amongst individuals, between organizations or between individuals and organizations and even nations. Often, betrayal is the act of supporting a rival group, or it is a complete break from previously decided upon or presumed norms by one party from the others. An act of betrayal creates a signature constellation, in both its victims and its perpetrators, of negative behaviors', thoughts, and feelings.

The interactions are complex. The victims exhibit anger and confusion, and demand atonement from the perpetrator; who in turn may experience guilt or shame, and exhibit remorse. If after the perpetrator has exhibited remorse or apologized, the victim continues to express anger, this may in turn cause the perpetrator to become defensive and angry in turn.

Acceptance of betrayal can be exhibited if victims forego the demands of atonement and retribution; but is only demonstrated if the victims do not continue to demand apologies, repeatedly remind the perpetrator or perpetrators of the original act, or ceaselessly review the incident over and over again. But when it comes to leadership especially at the leadership of salt of the earth the pay back to those betrayers is forgiveness. Offer just accordingly. Everyone suffers at least one bad betrayal in their lifetime. Look ahead to your leadership, those who promised you, to be there for you no matter what, Will eat their word, without hesitations.

As a time comes, to pay the leadership price .people who promised you, to be there in whatever comes up on you, may give their back, eat their words and work against you. Yes, they may betray you in time of need. Indeed. As a leader, you know where you are going. Don't let their betrayal, to put you in the middle of nowhere. Understand it, expect it and face bitter betrayal. Survive it. It's what unites us. The trick is not to let it to destroy your trust in others when that happens. Don't let them take your great faith and trust from you.

ASSASSINATION, MURDER, CRUSIFICATION

There may come the time, from a single individual to the groups all stand against you in the road to change Africa for the better. The leadership journey to saltine my people lives may be in question by others. It can be individuals or groups. Groups have often employed assassination as a tool to further their cause. Assassinations provide several functions for such groups, namely the removal of specific enemies and as propaganda tools to focus the attention of media and politics on their cause. The loss of your life inflicts enormous grief upon the individuals close to you and your followers. , the commission of a murder is highly detrimental or beneficial to those of my enemies within and outside.

Assassination is the murder of a prominent person or political figure by a surprise attack, usually for payment or political reasons. It may be prompted by religious, ideological, political, or military motives; it is an act that may be done for financial gain, to avenge a grievance, from a desire to acquire fame or notoriety, or because of a military or security services command to carry out the murder. In the just world, a person convicted of murder is typically given a long prison sentence, possibly a life sentence, life sentence where permitted, and in some countries, the death penalty may be imposed for such an act – though this practice is becoming less common, you will be imposed death penalty for nothing you do wrong but convey change to my people. Unjust law made my land lawless. The existing laws, works for the few interests not for the mass. Even the worst may happen, the one convicted of your murder or one who assassinates you might be considered hero as the eyes of my enemies and traitors at the eyes of your supporters. Depending on the jurisdiction, such circumstances may include: often punished more harshly, though you did not commit exceptional brutality or cruelty to my people, but you will be given slow and painful execution in which they tied or nailed you in a large wooden cross and left to hang until you dead.

It is often performed to terrorize and discourage its witnesses from perpetrating particularly monstrous crimes. Despite the fact that you are honestly attempts to serve my people and me. You commit not a single offense; you may be left on display as casualty after death as warnings to others who might attempt to follow your foot step. Remember any foot step to be salt of the earth for Mama Africa, leads you to pay even your priceless life. This act hastens your death but is also meant to deter those who observed the crucifixion from committing such act. You may be crucified or murdered but your spirits will live long in my land, don't be regretted, rather proud to pay such price and made up your mind to make me prestigious continent in the face of the world. But salt of the earth shall have the power of influence to survive murder and Crusification and killings. Cruel and disgusting punishments should be removed not only from an African body, but also from their mind. Crucifixion method varied considerably with location and time period. Those of my children's who stood to fulfill my heart desire were given various form of murder in different time differently. As others leaders of mine given bullets to their head and massacred at a day break and buried in mass. Therefore son, if any of my children love to see me civilized, be courageous to face death and drink the cup of it for me and for the next generations wellbeing. Carry on fighting for the emancipation of my people from cruel and disgusting punishments. I mean you give your valuable or priceless life for ransom to many.

UNPLEASING PEOPLE

To be beautiful means to be you. You don't need to be accepted by others. You need to accept yourself. Many of my people I live with feel that they have no joy in their life. They feel obligated to do so many things that they don't have time for themselves and the things they really want to do. As a result, they feel drained, anxious, and resentful.

With so many outside forces competing for their time, energy and financial resources, is it really any wonder they feel this way? So what does a leader do? How can salt of the earth remain balanced among this sea of obligations and commitments? You see my son; the answer is to live consciously. By looking at each decision we are making and by asking ourselves, "Is this really what I want to be doing? Is this really what is right for Africa?" And then by making sure our actions stay in alignment with our true intentions. Make sure Salt of the earth is a leader of his words. A true leader is a decision maker in every situation. The leader s YES is YES and NO is NO! I mean Real NO and real YES.

Saying YES when we mean NO often causes us not to trust ourselves. It damages our confidence and lowers our self-esteem. So why do we do it? From a young age, we are conditioned to act in certain ways in order to feel loved and accepted. This is the beginning of our loss of personal power and authenticity.

In order to create change we will need to recondition our beliefs by discovering what is really true for us. What is true for salt of the earth? Understanding resources are limited and human wants are unlimited. Having in mind serving to satisfy the need of my people will always be encountered with peoples unplanned and wishful thinking, wants accompanied with temporary fancies. So the duty of salt of the earth shall be satisfying the basic needs of my people and creating conducive environments for people to satisfy there need equally under the law. To make his responsibility get achieve, he shall be a decision maker. Decision shall not have a priority for things that weaken the moral of my people, things that violates my own unique cultures, act's that's against the good will of the mass and thoughts that forced me to live in poverty again. Thus, those of my children who want shortcut to happiness always shall not be happy by the decision of salt of the earth.

No matter how they hate him or unhappy about his carrier he ought to be ready not pleasing everyone in my land. Unpleasing people can occur at the road of true leadership. Fear of unpleasing people shall never lag you behind for stay true for your original vision and remain loyal to your mission in my land. It happens and ought to be survived. As it is one of the prices of leadership. But if you cannot survive unpleasing people, it means you are willing to stay short in the long walk to freedom. You may not be respected or loved by everyone in my land. That is true. But you shall continue your path to the new Africa. No matter how some people are unpleasant by your actions or thoughts. No matter how bad they feel about you and may disrespect you not fulfilling their greed. Be aware of any patterns and beliefs that no longer work for you and for me in my land. Once you become aware of these beliefs, you can simply commence to consciously change them. Changing people's thoughts and behavior is your major duty. Salt of the earth never works for his personal happiness and joy or dare to be accepted by others. Rather it is a mere fact, which rejection comes along in changing people's thoughts and actions. Since people thoughts and actions are not always positive. . Let me tell you son, the key to success which, I don't know but trying to please everybody is a start to failure in life. How come you please everybody? While you want to bless people then, ask you to do favor for their curse, devilish thoughts and actions. Are you going to do it? No .your job is different, to think different and do differently. Saying NO is a decision in my land.

You are not BRUSE ALMIGHTY to answer YES to

ALL questions asked.

Salt of the Earth never wants to be said "WHAT A NICE PERSON! " Or not eager to feel accepted; slightly exert positive influence power to have followers who, accepts his thoughts and actions. Yet, his thoughts and actions may contain YES or NO as necessary to get the job done. Remember you can choose differently. You can choose to believe you are valuable; what is right for you does matter, and that your happiness is not a priority. Your life is the culmination of each decision you make every moment (whether you are aware of what you are choosing or not). Begin to understand the intention behind every action you take and make a conscious decision to do only what is right for you as a visionary salt of the earth. What is right for mother Africa? What is right to African people?

Congregate the courage each moment and say "NO" to anything or anyone that doesn't allow you to be yourself, or to live in alignment with your dream. Dream to put me through the magnificent African form of civilization. What will you choose? Will you choose to stay in power by acting with the knowledge that you are responsible for every action in your life? Or will you continue to give your power away in order to feel valued and accepted in the eyes of another? The choice is yours. But Salt of the Earth survives the price of unpleasing people. Carry on it.

You see mama, now I got the big picture of it but seem hard to swallow?

I told you I no more cannot craft a superb future, by remaining stuck in my past. I need   leaders to cause me transformation and make my people life better. If one intends to do so, better to know how to get along with my people. So, it shall give you the way and formula of my heart desire and successes. To begin the road to new Africa, one shall make the end of my comfort zone now. It is the time to be there for me. It is time to set in motion. Life begins at the end of one's comfort zone. Because one will not win if don't begin. The journeys always make Salt of the Earth to pay leadership price. Beginning is half done. To sum up, one need to have the guts to be my Salt of my Earth and light my life. One shall decide to welcome all the challenges waiting.

Today's decisions are tomorrow's reality. There is always a danger that a leader burden burdened with responsibility for the man fold concern of the leader may knowingly or unknowingly veer in the direction of error in which case the honor and values of the leader will be at risk with undesirable consequences, for my people as a whole. In my land, bloods sweat and tears seems to be necessary to reach my dream, hope and joy. Make sure before you go through. If you want to be Salt of the Earth, always remember tough times never last but tough people do. Leadership is one long fight. The life of salt of the earth is full of fight. If you love, the people of Mama Africa, Be ready for a long fight. Every true leader goes the extra mile for his followers .going extra mile for people you love is never too much. You must carry on and carry through. Pay the price and remain alive after the challenge of life and your Salt of the Earth's service. When the storm is over Salt of the earth, stand still. Remain still, never back off. Eagles start flying to storm whiles other birds go back to their nests. Leaders shall live to fight the long fight of leadership. Survive in spite of danger.

You know some people who have a desire for money, power and fame? They intend to use the position of leadership to gain these things. Even My own children used me to meet their personal greed. That is not leadership of my heart desire.

They are fanatical to gain the prize of leadership, abstain themselves when it comes to pay the price. Salt of the earth is a journey to comforting others not comforting oneself. I was trying to point you only the common prices of salt of the earth. But the prices go beyond that. The long fight includes, being in crisis in your carrier. Huge rumors, pressure and High work load. You need to be extra committed. Selfless service always inquires to be one step ahead of my peoples thought and actions. Furthermore your unselfish service to my people In return, will invite physical and mental fatigue, beating by theirs, extreme exhaustions, and lots of pain, discrimination, and shipwreck and stoning. If you care about me, pay the leadership price for me!

CHAPTER FIVE

Why should one pay all this much at all mama? How can salt of the earth get the power and be able to pay?

You pay it for love, for the love of the people and everything in my land. Unconditional love gives you the power to face all the leadership challenges. Unconditional love fills you with power. The greatest power known to man is that of unconditional love. As humans, we have searched endlessly for the experience of love through the outer senses. Great nations have come and gone under the guise of love for their people.

If you do not have love, you can pay nothing for others, even for yourself too. Why should you? If you doesn't have respect for human beings, especially for those who were step aside of the cream of development in their own home land. You found yourself undecided to sacrifice. We pay it for love, for the love of the people. Unless we love and care about the people, how come we lead them? How could you serve me? How come you get the heart to pay the necessary leadership price, but if you are in love of the people unconditionally, you will indeed. Of course, you will have the courage and power to pay so. Son, Have you notice what the bible says about love?

I am not sure mama, will you?

Yes dear, it reads …

"Love gives you the power to do so. Love is patient. It is kind it does not envy, it does not boast, it is not proud. It does not dishonor others. It is not self-seeking, it is not easily Love doesn't delight in evil but rejoices with the truth. It always protects, always trusts, always hopes, and always perseveres. Love is not something we give or get; it is something that we nurture and grow, a connection that can only be cultivated among people. When it exists within each one of us – we can only love others as much as we love ourselves. Shame, blame, disrespect, betrayal, and the withholding of love damage the roots from which love grows. When they curse you, you will not revenge, fairly you bless. Even if they hassle and harass you, you will give them smile. When they mock at you, love makes you not to laugh at others and welcome their intolerance.

Through unconditional love you will make them tolerant and able to cut the edge of intolerance. By the way, intolerance by itself is violence. Love able you to stay true to your goal, love made you welcome the unwelcoming situation .love make the impossible possible. Love is a wonderful thing. Love makes you feel holy anger. This love is quite different. Its energy goes beyond mathematics, chemistry or physics. It is beyond politics.

Unconditional love drives you to see beyond tribe, race, and color, statuesque. It helps one to treat all the ugly black and the black beauty all equal. The short or the long blacks remain treated equally and fairly, simply humanly. Their tribe and skin color do not count in the eyes of salt of the earth. The haves and the have-nots shall be treated all equal under the law in my land.

Any leader, who rises in a basis of unconditional love, shall be willing to accept my people as they are. Unconditional love gives you the heart of great tolerance for those who are against or for. It will give you the limitless power to let it go, helps you to stand still no matter how difficult the journey of leadership becomes. This kind of love can make you stay loyal to your vision. Unconditional Love paves the way to unconditionally accept every single individual in my land and the rest of the world. These loves force you to be interested in people, in all people of all types and all races.

Salt of the earth unconditionally accept and cherish the value of others. Sees my children as equal and strives to bring out the best in everyone. If you love my people unconditionally, you can lead them. In return, they will be willing to go along to the direction you pointed them to go. Unconditional love exerts limitless power of influence. Unconditional love gives you the deeper strength that remains strong in every hurricane you face at all time. It will move your roots to go deeper and deeper in to people's heart. As storms make trees to have deep roots, every price you encountered in your leadership journey will make you have a strong forehead. Subsequently help you eagerly to welcome and face all the challenges and the challengers. The force of unconditional love will erase the doctrine of prejudice. In your delivery, no matter my children and other enemies of mine tries to   kick you out, insult, criticize, accuse, go against reject ,oppose , gossips behind ,spreads rumors, tells on bad stories, fabricates lies, drives you close to maddens, stooped you, hassle and try to kill you .no matter how people feel unpleased by your service, how they hated and make fun of you, how frequently betray and forsake you, how deliberately forged your careers, try to give you head to bullets and set fire on or else tries to put you on cross to exile or assassinate. Unrecognized your effort and despised your attitude and consciously ingratitude your service, ridicule and played your life.

As long as you are in love of humans unconditionally, you be capable of pay all the indispensable cost to save your motherland. Along with you will get the courage and the power to pay in the course of love. The power of love is held within each of us every moment. This wondrous energy is available merely by our use and conscious recognition. When we choose to love one another we transcend the lower personality perceptions and rise to a higher truth. We recognize our oneness, wholeness and interconnectedness. This is not a conditional love or the type of love one may try to use to earn favors or expect validation, rather this is a universal and unconditional love that recognizes the beauty in life every moment. It is of a higher nature. It is a natural expression that does not expect an outcome. It is giving just for the sake of giving. Bear in mind the journey of salt of the earth is serving others not self service.

It is in the sharing and giving of love to others that we receive the same that we give. Give love and surely you will experience love itself. Express love to the world around you and the world will reflect back to you the power of love. Of course, humanely speaking even as you encounter leadership challenges now and then, you get yourself at the end of your chapters of life and feel vexed. But so long as you have unconditional love for all your followers and enemies, you found yourself willing and ready to pay the entire price of leadership. On your salt of the earth journey, you shall possess incredible wisdoms and way outs to deal with all the challenge faced and the ups and downs waiting. Then found yourself ready to die in pain gladly.

Unconditional love will enhance you to live and die for the vision envisioned and make you willing to not accept the best dressed lies. Rather make you eager to die for the naked truth. Thus, be aware of only understanding truth, makes you liberate others. This love able you own worthwhile and meaningful life. Furthermore make you surrender your life for something greater than yourself. You sacrifice it for love. Headed for accomplishing your goal, leadership touch obstacles are inevitable.

In no way problem stops you, see problems have meanings to your leadership. Mama Africa has complex problems. If you see me just as problems only, you may be deficient in good will to help me. But if you see me as opportunity, you will be pleased and on no account overwhelmed. When we allow ourselves to understand the impact our actions have not only on ourselves but the planet we live on, we realize the necessity to take loving action. We each have the power to correct conditions within, as well as to affect the world we live in.

Forgiveness is the most powerful act of compassion you can make, both for you and others too. Mercy doings promotes unity. It is kindheartedness that transforms the old into the new.

This magnificent planet is filled with opportunities to experience love, deference, peace and joy. When we, as individuals, realize our potential to love unconditionally, we transform ourselves and the planet at the same time. Such is the power we wield every moment of every day. The choice is ours to craft a world of joy and happiness, love and goodwill. Living for others takes you to the high road. Make your mind up to take the high road. The walks of high road always make you to face challenges. All eyes are on you. So does my quest given that it is a call for not to be an ashtray of poor leadership. Living in an ashtray of poor leadership shall give you meaning to be my hero. My being an ashtray of poor leadership presents you an opportunity to initiate and lead change. Understanding the countless consequences of poor leadership will make you not to avoid any form of leadership in my land. As a leader it shall be better to recognize a problem before it becomes an emergency.

Good leaders predict and envisioned the future of Africa. If it seems a real problem to lag you behind, you better pay the price and survive it. Always remember we all have problems. Many of the salt of the earth are peoples who overcome problems in their life, yes we all have problems. But what matter is how we see it.

All what salt of the earth do is changing my children's perspective about the problem not their problems. Changing people's behavior and attitude may bring resistance to change. Through unconditional love you can make people to do what you want.

Yes, unconditional love reveals something more important - the individual potential that resides within each of us every moment. It merely asks that we approach each moment with clarity and right perspective and recognize the vast unlimited possibilities to choose a new way of thinking and feeling. Such a sense of profound love comes when we first forgive and accept ourselves for all our limiting beliefs, mistakes, judgments and misunderstandings and apply the "unconditional" to us personally as a leader. We recognize our self worth, value our talents, and allow ourselves to be who we are rather than what we think others wish us to be. In turn, we naturally understand those around us and extend our helping hand without condition, judgment or expectation. We see ourselves in the reflection of another and know that everyone deserves to love and be loved without condition. By embracing the present moment with openness we realize and know we have the solutions and answers already within us. We instigate building a reality that is based on love, wisdom and power in perfect balance. For each step we take personally, we impact the world with this amazing energy of love. As people who suffer lots of devastating life comings and goings, my people may want change in their lives but may not be willing to be changed. It is common in people when it comes to change. Due to lots of reasons they resist change. The change resistance might manifest in various forms, so be prepared to pay the price of leadership, while bringing something new to their lives. Though they may knowingly or unknowingly resist to the change idea, you shall stand vanguard to be their representation of change as a change catalyst and demonstrate what it means to be changed.

Truly change is something dangerous, it necessitate you come out of your comfort zone. My people lives look as if limited in their comfort zone. They seem not looking out of the box. This must be changed, as my heart desire quest. True leader understand unconditional love is an unlimited way of being.

We are without any limit to our thoughts and feelings in life and can create any reality we choose to focus our attention upon. There are infinite imaginative possibilities when we allow the freedom to go beyond our perceived limits. If we can dream it, we can build it. Life, in the course of unconditional love, is a wondrous adventure that excites the very core of our being and lights our path with sidelights. By the way, salt of the earth is light to the world. Currently my people live in the ashtray of poor leadership and feel adopt of its consequences. They are fearful to welcome extraordinary leadership at first. They accept to live with the known than the unknown. For that reason, it's up to the African salt of the earth to be the great symbol of change and open up his heart to lighten my life. Unconditional love turns hope into knowing in a collective reality that is often seen as hopeless or seemingly impossible to overcome.

May I know your expectation of your children might be?
What would they say expected to pay all the prices of
leadership for the sake of unconditional love?

I think my quest is a call of life and death. And I can imagine my children will send me letters to me back. That reads; - Dear mother we will never again let you down. You shall no more be an ashtray of poor leadership. You shall never die being poor. We shall neither see mama Africa die slowly nor walk slowly to die in our youth. At golden times of our youth life, never again avoid our responsibilities. We understand the secret of greatness is pursuing our responsibility. We will be your loyal servant children and shall pay the necessary price, no matter how difficult it would be. We pay it for love to you, our brothers and sisters. Their life is our life their death is our death.

We respect, honor and accept your quest. Shall try our best never dare to eat our words. And we will have the courage to do so and unconditionally do it for the sake of love. Love for Africans humanity.

No matter how our past tries to lag us behind. Whatever our current situations are prevailing, nothing will stop us, except death. We understand death is inevitable, and we all are mortal .but never again our death became ordinary; rather die honorable offering selfless service to make the long walk of your freedom short. We will be salt of the earth, and bless everything on our motherland. Will knee your enemies and shall never touch you again mama. Never, never again remain silent and irresponsible looking our mother Africa at the edge of graveyard. You will flourish like day light; your prosperity will be decorated in African form of civilization at the expense of your youth Mama Africa.

Very positive of you!

Of course I am whatever good or bad they did to me, they are still my children. I love them unconditionally. We cultivate love when we allow our most vulnerable and powerful selves to be deeply seen and known, and when we honor the spiritual connection that grows from that offering with trust, respect, kindness and affection. Children do what parents' do. If you give love to them, they pay you love in return. Along with, Love will bestow them all the passion to have holy anger, not to see me failed and broken hearted again. My children shall essentially be filled in righteous anger. Every salt of the earth as well expected to have it.

I haven't heard of it, Earlier you told me love is not easily angered. What kind of anger is Righteous anger?

It is not as that of natural fleshly anger. It is different. Whilst one gets angry of something positively, Holy anger doesn't drive you to commit sin. It is the different anger that rises within you against wickedness in my continent. It is against injustice, oppression, Inequality, illiteracy, poor governance and male administration, etc. If things go wrong in my land, Salt of the earth shall have holy anger. Whilst holy anger comes up on you, as a leader you are expected to take certain decisions. Unless otherwise, things in my land will continue as is. Its consequences are limitless. Therefore my children's must need to have the courage and willingness to get angry in their wickedness. It is honorable anger against devilish thoughts and actions. It is Harmless and blessed anger to make things right and do things right. It is anger against mismanagement, poor leadership and irresponsibility and inappropriateness.

What will happen, either salt of the earth or your children lack the courage to feel holy anger in their life? And unable to unconditionally love and cherish each other?

God forbid that, but if my children unable to love and cherish each other , For the rest of my life and entire land will be an ashtray, ashtray of poor leadership. An ashtray full of bloodbath nakedness ,lie , subjugation ,favoritism ,slavery, sorrow, famine ,drought, , hatred, jealousy, rumor disease, illiteracy, scandal, humiliation, slum, sob, homelessness, sin, theft, murder, wildness, corruption, pessimism and obscurity.

A continent full of Losers, Jovian delinquency, inhumanity, brutality, cruelty, terrorism, anxiety ,resentment ,unlimited migration, crime, ignorance, disaster, disorder, injustice ,over pollution, desertification, Grief, guilt, hypocrisy, intolerance, scarcity of resource, Idleness, greediness, and joblessness, I can't count the limitless consequences.

With the intention that, I insist my children be aware of certain extent about the ugliness of an ashtray of poor leadership. Its consequences will notify not to be unfortunate, flunky leaders and inform you the irresponsible wipe out of all the natural and human resources, which brings the discomfort of our unborn children. Misusing is mismanagement. That is poor leadership. If we don't question things in and outside and accept for granted as is, is willingly accept its effects that has in it.

How can you get if you don't ask. Accepting everything without questioning is not modernization in 21st century, somewhat is ignorance. The choice is up to my children to live prosperous or grievous. Unwilling and avoiding not to feel righteous anger and not to cherish unconditional love for one another in my land means you prefer to live in post modernization era without modernization. Everything depends on the leadership.

"No good leader no development"

Poor leadership exerts curse. My children shall never let poor leadership spoil their priceless life. It would be fair thinking about me as your aged mother whose nose long for the smell of successes.

My eyes need to see my ancient civilization to revive again. Unless and otherwise my children are not willing to have righteous anger and not responsible of their thoughts and actions, the ashtrays of poor leadership will drive me to my dead end as is. It shall make me dig my own graveyard. And trapped me stay short of my long hope to be a prosperous and well civilized continent.

Before I sum up my question, wonder to know how you are felling these days?

As you see me I found myself in the middle of nowhere!!! In my entire life I had been all the way through up and downs, had been married and divorced quite a lot.

What could you call it such a life?

DYING SLOWLY OR SLOWLY DYING!!

I am feeling a mother who dares to live an African indigenous motherhood, but act differently. I feel vexed, Yearning to see my children one day save my life.

How on earth your children can survive all the price of salt of the earth?

Every child of mine all over the world who hear my quest of salt of the earth , willing and ready to offer their priceless life joyfully for my continental call, for sure will understand my heart desire and words and shall put it in to practice ,will build my house on the rock. The rain came down, the streams rose, and the winds blew and beat against that house; yet it did not fall, because it had its foundation on the rock. Winds shape mountains. Storm makes trees to have deep roots. So does a true African leader survive every single leadership difficulties? A true African leader laid its foundation on the rock, never build it on sand. If he does so, he inwardly understands every single challenges beats against the house, and it fell with a great crash. Therefore one survives the entire price through building my house on the rock.

WHY NOW?

Many efforts have been made and fine initiatives have been developed in the past for my development. But most have failed for different reasons. According to my life experience some of the main reasons for past failures concerning of leadership are lack of genuine political will. Political determination took the lion share.

Why now Mama?

In spite of everything, am now at a critical juncture in history. Unless and otherwise, I firmly get in touch with my children as it should be as a mother, encompassing Africanized form of civilization is at risk. Thus, the tragedy of my people common agenda for the united and civilized Africa need to redeemed. Our African daily routines exemplify the need to make new history by

Africans. An African problem deserves an African solution. By then I conceive thought to have great African salt of the earth among my children, and came up with a decision. This put me on emergency to have salt of the earth. Above all this, my guts told me .it's the time for Africa! , it's time for Africa even to bless the world with unspeakable richness.

The newly seen initiatives of my children show me ripe conditions for the understanding, realizing and releasing African potential. I am convinced if I get in touch with my children as it should be right now, no doubt at all, they will firmly grasp this unique opportunity. The present relative goodwill and momentum must be maintained.

The implementation of my quest for salt of the earth should proceed without delay.

In the name of my children bloods and bones, I tell you, I CAN NOT AFFORD TO FAIL FOR THE SAKE OF FUTURE GENERATIONS. I can't stand my own children despise and disgrace me and the rest of us at the face of this civilized world.

It's time to   change and   genuinely committed to develop critical mass of leadership within meant for the renaissance of my people' life and entire land.   The commitments shall never again be externally imposed or driven but shall be in my own interest. After five decades of independence and development efforts, most of my people are poorer than they were in the early 60s. Development assistance mainly from the west has not produced the desired change in the quality of lives of my people.

Lack of good governance, poor leadership in addition to debt burden, corruption and etc were the daily wake up call to me. The predicament of my people has forced me to take a new and critical look at the development scene of my land. Therefore, I persist intentionally to release a pressing duty to my people so as to eradicate poverty, Place their countries in order, both individually and collectively, on the path of sustainable growth and development simultaneously. I no more be measured by the opinions of others. I understand my potential is limitless. I possess the ability to develop, accomplish, produce, create and perform anything my mind can conceive.

If I am mistaken I will be corrected Mama but it seems.
Dreams of a multi-cult utopia that have been achieved
nowhere are you hopeful on what you quest?

I am not surprised of what you think of, let me tell you one
of my great son once told me "it seems impossible until it
gets done" in despite of my current situation ,long ago my
African children have made things which the world still
wonders about, in times of were no technology at all. They
have survived what it seems impossible even now.

I have big hope to have true and extraordinary leaders of
my heart desire. One is that I have great hope on those
African hands that built my ancient civilization, will revive
again. It's time to reclaim those brilliant minds, who
crafted the world UNESCO registered African heritages.
And the new generation will again build the new Africa
with the new African spirit followed by my Quest.

I am curious to offer my African leaders the unique
formula for progress. After experiencing holy anger and
unconditional love within, hope to share to the rest of the
world.

Oh son my frustration not having a true salt of the earth
seemed to drive me close to madness. And you may
consider my quest as a dream of a multi-cult utopia. The
naked black children of mine had to answer for.

In reality what I need is to find a way for each of my culture to meet its own aspirations. And it is possible, no matter how easier said than done. Hence, what on earth the realization of my dream take, I will not give up.

Forcing transformation down my throats won't work. It will just breed resentment. I want to know what's best for a poor mother like me. Should I keep abused and let others brought abuse raining down on me? Or be hopeful to get some to rely on? Actually, I have both the hopes and dreams. I no more marvel at my luck of development and the level of my poverty. Of course I have a dream one day I may not need loan, may not stretch my hand to beg, and may not see foreign company to build toilets (infrastructures) for me.

There may not be much sickness and suffering, and Will achieve stable and prosper nation created by Africans. For sure my people will set their own system of governance. They will set and maintain African measurement ways of standards, quality and excellence for each and everything Africans life contain. My children's will not develop a sense of suspicion for their own products, will audaciously pay the necessarily respect for local products and indigenous systems of administration and institutionalization. I can imagine the well trained, confident competent, skilled and most beloved African leaders of all times. I can envision   my children have the emancipation to dominate their environment and become truly free. I hope my children's will know who truly they are and accept it without plus or minus and experience freedom with great responsibility.   In spite of my circumstances, I shall stay positive and cling to my hope high to get leaders of my heart desire. My quest is exceptionally practical not imaginary.

Mama, are you saying you are no more in need of outside help?

Before you say "I need this and that," you need to know why you need something and you don't. Don't you? Only the wearer knows where the shoe pinches.

A baby carried on his mother back cannot understand how far and difficult the road is by itself. Depending on others does not guardant once future. Relaying on yourself and your own resource increase your self esteem and sustain self empowerments. In fact, the rest of the world tries their best to give their hand and solve my problem. Thanks for those who truly gave me hands. But most of them offered their help within their hidden agenda. Still they describe their hidden agenda with anodyne phrases such as development, investments, employment generations and so forth. Their elongated hand still made me feel down, and foreigner unfair engagement is dwarfed by those of my reluctant children. Though am not saying I am in need of outside help no more absolutely, of course I need differently.

I ought to have two-way kinds of help, which sustain my development and benefit me mutually with the rest of the world. I may not be mouthful to say, I need no one by my side, I will be out of the globalization game. It is undeniable No nation can stand without the other. We need each other. For instance let me give you an idea about how this happen. Though every continent independently able to pressure and maintain their environments, I am dependent on the developed world for environmental preservation, on which hopes for sustainable development depend.

Of course, Global warming is harming both the developed ones and I. We both accumulated and even current green house gas emissions still predominantly originate from the high income countries. Thus, I endure environmental dependence, which I must rely on the Developed world to cease aggravating the problem and to develop solutions. To do so, I shall work in co-operation with the rest of the world for mutual benefit.

Beside the decisive local environmental solutions I must develop. Moreover, my continental call is all about bringing the very far very close. During times of debt crisis the interests of international banks often prevailed over those of desperately indebted nations, like that of me.

Unless I have strong bargaining positions than developed nations, I remain left weaker bargaining positions in international economic relations. The economic development expansion behavior depends on universal development. Therefore, I shall closely work with them, to advance my economy and became a good bargaining nation. Not only for this reasons, I shall work with them to bring the promised but has still been too slow and sub stated debt relief to remain not vulnerable going forward. And I shall work closely and cooperatively with the rest of the world due to my inner conviction of every community has something to share and something to gain.

Finally Mama, would you like to leave some message to your children?

Yes dear, dear my children all over the world. Please be informed your mother is at the junction of history.

I am sick and tired of my own vampire children. I can't afford for my own vampire leaders who prey ruthlessly on others. I tell you, mama Africa can't afford for bloodsucking African leaders. Generally speaking ,my quest for Salt of the Earth ,is to maintain the broken, smoothening the rough road, lightening the dark, Healing the wounded, meeting the unmated, bringing the far closed, purring the polluted, clearing the contaminated, tidying the slum, tapping the untapped, seeking knowledge and applying it effectively, flourishing the hidden, unlocking the locked., nothing more nothing less.

This is my heart desire. No more to be broken spirit. I badly need my peace extended like river and wealth like flooding stream. Take heart. Stand still, rejoined your daily life responsibly, search then for your strength -- for your largeness of spirit -- somewhere inside yourself. I have a faith in you. My faith will heal me. Whilst you answer my quest cheerfully, that time, you will nurse me. Please courageously carry on Put my enemies under my foot.

Especially those false profits, leaders of mine came in shipping clothes, but inwardly who are ferocious wolves.
Let you out of me shall came and became African Salt of the Earth. I kindly beg you with tears in,   from the bottom of my heart, being naked and had been as naked society. Am I not a mother of a billion? Am I not known of being a cradle of human being?

Please for God's sake!

Don't make me a barren mother!

THE END

ABOUT THE AUTHOR

Yohannes Tassew is motivational speaker, author and translator and globally connected and locally engaged active citizen master facilitator. Was gyp (glocal youth parliamentarian). Is an industrious and resourceful community developmental practitioner, with 12 years experience in civic leadership , has high emotional intelligence. He has served as....President- Yekatit 12 Preparatory School Student Council-2003-2005

V/ President-Addis Ababa University College of Commerce Student Union, 2007
GYP Glocal Youth Parliamentarian -Delegating Ethiopian Youth-Glocal Forum.2006-2008
V- President-Addis Ababa Youth Federation-2008
Project Coordinator and Chef Volunteer Facilitator-Addis Ababa Youth Association-2008-2009
President-Addis Ababa Youth Association-2010-2013
President-Addis Ababa Youth Federation 23 July 2009-23 April 2011
Executive Committee Ethiopian Youth Federation 2009-2011
V/President-Ethiopia Youth Federation-2012- Up to Date and travel for seminaries in Africa and Europe.

Yohannes Has Play Therapy Skills certification of attendance a- diploma level from play therapy international, approved by international board of examiners of child and play therapy. . And he is appreciative inquiry (AI) practitioner. He is 30. Currently he is living young as a full time author and inspirational/motivational speaker in Addis Ababa Ethiopia.

www.ingramcontent.com/pod-product-compliance
Lightning Source LLC
Chambersburg PA
CBHW050449290526
45786CB00006B/2220